SPIRITUAL
TRANSFORMATION

SPIRITUAL
TRANSFORMATION

12 Steps to Freedom,
Joy, and Your Highest Life

Dr. K Narayan

Copyright © 2025 by K Narayan, Ph.D.

All rights reserved. No part of this book may be reproduced or used in any manner without the written permission of the copyright owner, except for the use of quotations in a book review. For more information, contact: inquiry@spiritual-transformation.org

First print edition October 2025

ISBN 978-1-966026-01-3 (paperback)
ISBN 978-1-966026-00-6 (hardcover)

www.spiritual-transformation.org

To the Light within
That strives
Lifetime after lifetime
To master the human game

TABLE OF CONTENTS

Introduction: *My Transformation Journey and an Invitation* 9

Step 1. Upgrade Your Beliefs 21
Gerry's Journey 47

Step 2. Accelerate Your Spiritual Evolution 51
Suzy's Journey 70

Step 3. Detoxify and Disconnect 75
DeBorah's Journey 91

Step 4. Channel Higher Energies 95
Adela's Journey 110

Step 5. Cultivate Daily Spiritual Practice 113
Joanna's Journey 129

Step 6. Align with Soul Purpose 133
Daniel's Journey 147

Step 7. Grow and Take Risks 151
Mary's Journey 162

Step 8. Honor Your Time, Attention, and Money 167
Sara's Journey 189

Step 9. Transform Your Health 193
Brenda's Journey 203

Step 10. Transform Your Relationships ... 207
Claire's Journey ... 222

Step 11. Pursue Joy ... 227
Stefenie's Journey ... 235

Step 12. Serve ... 239

Conclusion: Become an Instrument of Light ... 251
Appendix: The Lightworker's Journey ... 255
References ... 259
About Children of Infinity ... 266
About Dr. K Narayan ... 267

Introduction: My Transformation Journey and an Invitation

What is spiritual transformation, and why should you desire it?

The word *trans-formation* denotes a change in form so radical that it transcends mere improvement or adaptation. When a caterpillar transforms, it undergoes a period of apparent destruction and re-formation. In the end, it emerges not as a better caterpillar but a butterfly, a fundamentally different creature. What once was a dull, earthbound creature has now developed wings to fly and radiate beauty.

Transformation is not merely growth—it is rebirth.

Physical transformation, such as that of a caterpillar, is genetically informed and unavailable to humans. All of us, however, bear within the potential for *spiritual transformation*—a profound process of shedding old identity, beliefs, and patterns to reveal an empowered, expansive self. The inner rebirth enables us to transcend limitations, connect with our true purpose, and live a meaningful, joyous life.

Spiritual transformation is not an exclusive privilege of mystics or ascetics; rather, it is a universal journey that calls to each of us, inviting us to explore our deepest essence and awaken our revolutionary potential. This book is an invitation to embark on that journey—a journey transcending religion, culture, and dogma. It speaks to the essence of what it means to be human. In this book, I will share timeless principles and practical tools to guide you.

Before we set out on this path together, however, let me share how my own journey has unfolded.

My Journey of Spiritual Transformation

On my spiritual path, I have observed that there are long periods of imperceptible growth, times when nothing seems to happen, interspersed with great leaps in consciousness—*awakenings* that herald immense changes. I have experienced *five* such awakenings.

My first awakening happened in 1996, when I was a sixteen-year-old boy in India. My life's purpose changed when I read *Autobiography of a Yogi* by the enlightened master Paramahansa Yogananda. The book ended my socially programmed search for validation and symbols of success, inspiring me instead to seek *enlightenment*.

Growing up in a small town, however, I had neither guidance nor the means to pursue enlightenment. Although I had little freedom for this pursuit as a high schooler, I knew that enlightenment was about going beyond the conditioned self and the suffering it creates. Driven by inner guidance, I began to read voraciously about consciousness and the nature of existence. I also started to meditate daily.

In the beginning, my meditations were simple: I would sit quietly, try to calm my mind, and focus on my breath. My teenage mind rebelled against the practice, but the struggle subsided in a few months. Meditation enabled me to focus my mind and do well in studies. After high school, I passed an extremely competitive nationwide exam to enroll at the Indian Institute of Technology, Bombay (IITB), to pursue an engineering degree.

The years at IITB were invaluable for my intellectual growth. I had the opportunity to interact with India's brightest minds, and I received outstanding training in technology. This was also my first exposure to the English-speaking world, and I soon fell in love with Western classical music, literature, and, most importantly, physics. In a course on relativity, I and my fellow students were astonished to learn that space and time can stretch! A course on quantum mechanics taught us that fundamental particles—the very building blocks of reality—are not things but rather waves of probability affected by observers. Physics offered a pathway for me to reconcile my spiritual understanding with a well-studied model of reality. Inspired, I switched my major to engineering physics and began studying theoretical physics.

After receiving my undergraduate degree in 2003, I was accepted by the University of Texas at Austin to pursue graduate studies in physics. Adjusting to a new country and culture was challenging, but being in a new intellectual environment and learning the foundations of quantum physics provided the philosophical framework I needed to complement my spiritual experiences. Quantum physics gave me a scientific perspective on spirituality—one based on energy and the quantum field rather than religion. While I was still a graduate student, I reached another significant milestone: in 2008, I met and married Aditi.

In 2009, one year before receiving my Ph.D., I felt inwardly guided to learn computer programming. I took a few courses and found the subject fascinating. Programming offered me something that theoretical physics did not—craftsmanship. I could *build* software and then *tweak* it infinitely. After I finished the programming courses, I attended the campus job fair at UT Austin. A Fortune 20 corporation did an on-the-spot interview with me, then invited me to a more in-depth interview. After four rounds of interviews, they offered me a job. As I meditated on my path forward, I was guided to bid farewell to the academic world. Although I did not understand it at the time, it turned out that working within a corporation would provide me with the best opportunity to develop the leadership skills I would need a decade later.

After graduation, my wife and I moved to New York City to start a new life, and I, my dream job. The initial months as a software developer were exciting, with numerous opportunities to learn and excel. As the months progressed, however, a strange discontent began to build within me. I felt that the long hours I spent building financial software were utterly meaningless. As my restlessness grew, I began questioning my path: *What was I doing with my life?* Had I exchanged my once all-consuming search for enlightenment for a salary and a comfortable life? Had the seeker within perished? Feeling lost, I also became seriously depressed.

I later understood that I was undergoing a spiritual crisis—a difficult yet necessary phase that often precedes a breakthrough. As my desperation grew into a deep longing for meaning, the raging fire eventually led to my *second* awakening: In 2011, I experienced a *kundalini* awakening.

Kundalini is a primal intelligence that is present in every human being. It has dual aspects. Its physical aspect—the intelligence of the DNA—is active in all of us and develops the body-mind. The spiritual aspect, however, stays dormant until it is awakened through sincere seeking and spiritual practice. A kundalini awakening is similar to receiving the seed of enlightenment, though work still needs to be done to nurture it for full harvest.

That awakening profoundly changed my inner experience. Before the awakening, my meditation was focused on the mind and its creations, such as thoughts. After the awakening, I became aware of what *creates* the mind: energetic patterns lying below conscious awareness. I could feel energy moving through my body and creating a tingling sensation in my spine. Ineffable peace came over me.

For several days, I lived on the edge of physical existence, sleeping only a few hours a day and eating a fraction of my normal diet. Although the physical effects eventually wore off, the peace stayed. My depression lifted, even though my job had not changed. I felt alive and on purpose again, having finally received the energetic seed of enlightenment I had sought for fifteen years! Now, I only needed to tend it to fruition.

For the next eight years, I dove more deeply within, while the outer aspects of my life unfolded effortlessly. Our marriage was happy, and my wife and I had two children. I managed the pressure and obligations of my job successfully and was promoted. Content, I decided I would focus primarily on spiritual practice for the rest of my life. Life, however, had other plans.

In late 2019, I felt an urgent call to begin sharing my spiritual knowledge with others. At first, I tried to ignore that call. I wondered: *Is this a trick of my ego, trying to tempt me away from my spiritual practice? Why get distracted from my lofty goal?*

But the call persisted and forced me to introspect. I realized that the true source of my avoidance was fear. I had poor communication skills, spoke with a heavy Indian accent, and had not created a distinguishing body of work to establish myself as an expert. Why would anyone listen to an engineer like me talk about *spirituality?* What would I even share? And how? I also faced practical limitations: managing a software team and raising two young kids left me with little time or mental energy to spare.

Amidst the inner struggle, I saw that the call was an invitation to my *third* awakening—becoming a spiritual teacher. Although I still suffered from deep insecurity, inaction was no longer an option.

I surrendered to the call and asked for inner guidance. I was led to take a small first step by creating an online community on Meetup.com and setting up a webinar to share spiritual insights. Part of me still felt reluctant and hoped no one would show up, but a few dozen people did attend the first gathering. One man had undergone a near-death experience (NDE) and needed guidance to integrate it. As the evening unfolded, people wanted to hear more about my perspective, and they encouraged me to organize my thoughts into a body of teaching.

Only in hindsight do I understand why the call was so strong. Within two months of that first meeting, the COVID pandemic hit. The world shut down, and people were forced to go within. As virtual communication became the norm, I began reaching a global audience and realized that millions of people could benefit from a scientific model of spirituality.

As I realized that I needed to enlarge my mission from that of achieving personal enlightenment to that of humanity, I eventually created Children of Infinity, a nonprofit dedicated to raising planetary consciousness. I began offering video courses and study groups to make spiritual education freely and widely available.

After I chose to devote the remaining years of my life to a greater cause, I experienced the next phase in my growth—unlocking my spiritual gifts. I knew as a teacher that *transformation requires technology, not merely knowledge*. My quest for spiritual technology led me to mystics who can tap directly into the Source Dimension—the vast energy field of Consciousness—and can channel energy into the Physical Dimension. If you have seen *The Matrix*, there is a scene in the movie where Trinity learns to fly a helicopter *instantly* by downloading the flying program into her brain. As incredible as it may seem, this is not merely science fiction—this is how reality is structured! There is a constant transfer of information and energy from the Source Dimension (true reality) to the Physical Dimension (simulated reality, or the "matrix").

The concept that we live in a simulated reality is not new. Thousands of years ago, Eastern mystics called this concept *Maya;* scientists today use the term *simulation hypothesis*. While science postulates the existence of the Source Dimension, it does not yet possess the technology to harness energy from that dimension, because contemporary science still focuses on the material—not spiritual—aspect of existence.

Mystics through the ages, however, have possessed the ability to tap into the Source Dimension. My quest for spiritual technology led me to such a mystic—John Chandler. John is a direct disciple of Maharishi Mahesh Yogi, the teacher who originated the Transcendental Meditation movement. When I met John in 2020, he had been on the spiritual path for more than half a century. He had achieved such a high state of consciousness that he was working with the core energies of creation, including Divine Mother, the feminine aspect of Source.

To be honest, I felt skeptical when John told me that he worked with Divine Mother. Because of my limiting beliefs, I could not imagine that a human being could work with the divine. I thought the best a human being could do was to *pray* to the divine—and hope the prayers were heard. Fortunately, John offered a class that helped me directly experience Divine Mother's energy. After that experience, I accepted him as my teacher. Even as I continued teaching to my own growing community of students, I dedicated myself to learning everything John had to offer.

I spent the next years learning from John and working with powerful initiations from Divine Mother. Through John's guidance and Divine Mother's grace, I experienced my *fourth* awakening—the ability to transmit Divine Mother's energy through my voice, similar to how a wire transmits electricity. Using the energy, I began creating meditations that serve as energetic tools for transformation. The reason these tools are so effective is that their energy works at a level below the mind and therefore can heal deeply embedded programs, which are called *samskaras* in the yogic tradition. Similar to the software running a computer, samskaras run our lives. Changing these programs leads to remarkable results. For example, Tim, a member of our community, had been drinking since he was seventeen. At age sixty-three, after a few weeks of daily practice with the "Stairway of Light" meditation (see Step 5), he lost the desire to drink. Other community members have finally relinquished addictions to smoking or food, and have quit other unhealthy patterns such as having persistent anger.

As my work with Divine Mother's energy continued, in 2023 I realized that to transform planetary consciousness, we need thousands of lightworkers—people devoted to raising their consciousness and helping others do the same. The quest to empower lightworkers led to my *fifth* awakening—becoming a leader.

During times of crisis, leaders act as catalysts and inspire the next generation of leaders. Regrettably, we have few models of authentic spiritual leadership today. To help fill the void, I have established Leaders of Light, a coalition of leaders possessing both a strong desire and the skills needed to facilitate planetary transformation. To create a worldwide movement of Light, I empower leaders not only with training and guidance but also with energetic tools from Divine Mother. As people with a critical mass devote themselves to planetary transformation, one day, not too far into the future, we will create a conscious, compassionate, and joyous planet.

An Invitation to Your Own Transformation Journey

Human civilization has evolved to the point where most people's physical needs are met. Abraham Maslow, a pioneer of research on psychological health, believed human needs are hierarchical: the lower needs—security and survival—come first; then come the psychological needs—for stability and success. When these are secured, only then can humanity seek to fulfill its higher needs, or self-actualization, which Maslow considered the pinnacle of human existence. While only a privileged few could pursue self-actualization in the past, today the conditions are ripe for a mass movement that will herald the elevation of consciousness on our planet.

The Onion of Transformation

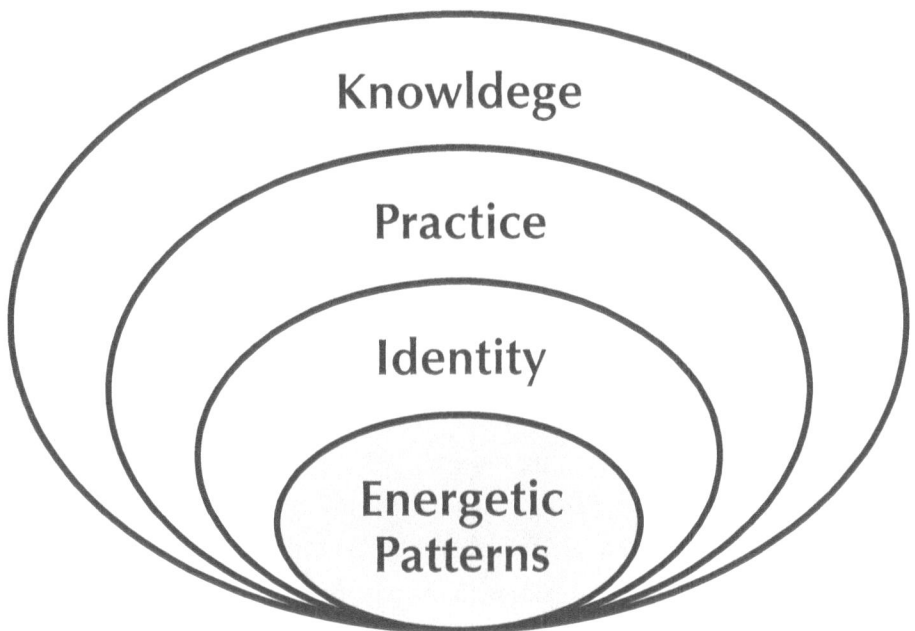

I have found that transformation is like an onion consisting of layers you peel back as you evolve. Each layer represents deeper growth.

The outermost layer, **knowledge,** shapes your model of reality. Lacking the correct model is like trying to push open a locked door without using a key. No matter how hard you push, the door will remain closed.

While knowledge is important, intellectual concepts alone will not lead you to a direct experience of higher consciousness. What you need is the second layer: **practice.** Just as a pianist must practice daily to create beautiful music, you must practice to master your mind—the powerful instrument that creates your reality. The goal is to cultivate a mind that radiates peace and joy, regardless of life's conditions.

The third layer is **identity**, where you see yourself as an empowered spiritual being. Your identity shifts from victim to creator and, eventually, to *lightworker*. The lightworker nurtures the inner light that later radiates outward, inspiring others.

The deepest layer of transformation occurs at the level of one's **energetic patterns,** or *samskaras*. These deep-rooted programs are the software that runs your life. Imagine owning a computer with bugs. No matter what upgrades you make to the computer, the software will keep creating unwanted results. Similarly, we humans have accumulated limiting patterns that create unwanted tendencies, behaviors, and habits. Since these are energetic in nature, the most efficient way to correct them is with energy.

Our planet is undergoing an energetic upgrade, and the number of people with an elevated consciousness is higher than ever before. Therefore, energetic seeds are available to seekers without the need for the elaborate preparations and purifications that once were practiced in the yogic tradition. In this book, I will show you how to effectively use the new spiritual technology.

About This Book and How to Use It

This book is born from a Children of Infinity community quest designed to facilitate spiritual transformation. Taking a holistic view of the human journey, the quest focuses not only on consciousness and meditation but also on other important aspects—health, finances, relationships, and alignment with Soul Purpose. Undertaken with peers who offer support and accountability, the quest offers a transformative framework of knowledge, practice, and community. Given that the quest size is limited, however, I wrote this book to make spiritual transformation accessible to a broader audience.

This book serves as a guide for the 12-step process toward spiritual transformation. Each chapter in the book features one transformative step as well as exercises to integrate learning with action. Move through these steps sequentially, at least through the book's first half.

I recommend getting a dedicated journal to immerse yourself in the book's teachings. Use the journal as your companion for reflection, inquiry, and keeping a record of your spiritual progress. Ideally, also find one person to take this journey with you—a fellow student with whom you may share fellowship and insights. If you are unable to find a fellow student, however, you can still achieve results through deep engagement with the material. Complete all the exercises, and follow a daily routine for learning and practicing.

An Important Note

To learn about the numerous facets of transformation, I have interviewed dozens of people: teachers, nonprofit leaders, university professors, retirees, and entrepreneurs. In this book, I feature stories from twelve such people to underscore that spiritual transformation happens to seekers from *all* walks of life, not merely to monks meditating for long hours in remote monasteries. I have strived to present each person's viewpoint without alteration.

As a reader, it is natural that you will find some of these views in harmony with your beliefs—and others not. I request that you view each individual compassionately. Further, two points are worth emphasizing:

1. Some of the interviewees express a disparaging view of religion, which might differ from your own view. I encourage you to reflect on your experiences and form your own perspective, while remaining open to learning from the experiences of others.

2. I have met these individuals through Children of Infinity, the nonprofit I founded. Many of them credit the organization for their spiritual transformation. This book, however, is not meant to be a promotional tool, only an informative one.

I hope you find the featured stories helpful on your spiritual path.

Welcome to the journey from being earthbound to learning how to soar!

Step 1: Upgrade Your Beliefs

As long as the attack is upon effects only, rather than causes, no change is possible. If a factory is torn down but the rationality which produced it is left standing, then that rationality will simply produce another factory.

—Robert Pirsig

The path of least resistance and least trouble is a mental rut already made. It requires troublesome work to undertake the alteration of old beliefs.

—John Dewey

Spiritual transformation sounds like a big change. And it is.

So—where do you start?

That bit is straightforward. You start by changing your worldview. Let's define exactly what that is.

Your worldview is an underlying model of reality that explains the universe and your place in it. Constructed from a set of related, interconnected beliefs, your worldview fashions the very fabric of your existence. This is because it both governs how you see reality and answers the pivotal question: *What is the meaning and purpose of human existence?*

Think of your worldview as the foundation of a house, with its floors, walls, doors, windows, and roof constructed upon that foundation. Your worldview forms the bedrock of your existence and helps you make sense of the human journey. Should that foundation be unstable or uneven, or have gaps, the building that sits upon it will not be secure.

Your worldview began forming in early childhood and has been shaped by a complex interplay of influences—culture, family, education, life events, media, and many others. If you haven't consciously examined your beliefs, the most significant factor shaping your worldview may simply be where you were born. There's a good chance that you believe what your parents believed and that your children, if you have any, will be brought up to believe what you believe.

When you react positively or negatively to a situation, your beliefs are always at play. You create a narrative about a person or event that fits your belief system, but the story you tell yourself may or may not be true. Consider an everyday example:

> Alex and Kai are experiencing trouble in their friendship. When Alex brings this up with Kai, Kai refuses to talk and retreats into silence. Alex has encountered this pattern of behavior in a previous friendship and believes *Kai does not value their relationship.* As a

result of his beliefs, Alex has formed an explanation that feels true. But is it true? Perhaps…perhaps not, but Alex is unlikely to consider the possibility that his beliefs may be wrong.

Many of us suffer because of our limiting beliefs, which are hard to change because they have become an inseparable part of our identity. Yet, to unlock our highest life, we must shed these dysfunctional mental models, just as we discard old tools that no longer serve us and old clothes that no longer fit us.

When our beliefs change, new possibilities become available. Consider the world of medicine: for centuries, it was believed that epilepsy was caused by evil spirits. We now know that this condition arises from neurological issues. Only by abandoning a disempowering myth once regarded as fact have we as a race developed effective treatments for epilepsy and improved the quality of life for those affected by it.

This same principle applies to spiritual growth: progress begins when we challenge the "truths" that hold us back. No matter how deeply held your beliefs may be, there are almost always more empowering alternatives waiting to be discovered. Upgrading your beliefs enables you to move through life with greater ease, clarity, and effectiveness. History's greatest breakthroughs—both personal and collective—stem from recognizing the following key insights about beliefs:

- All beliefs, no matter how deeply entrenched, are mere *assumptions* about reality.

- Beliefs are *choices,* and never objective facts.

- A rational approach requires first examining our beliefs for correctness and then consciously seeking better beliefs. To cultivate such *thinking about thinking* is not only useful—it's a central aim of human evolution.

You can upgrade your worldview by stepping back, viewing the bigger picture, and examining your core beliefs about reality. The inquiry will help you understand how your beliefs have created your current worldview, which in turn determines how you live your life. Let's do an exercise to explore your core beliefs.

EXERCISE
Examine Your Worldview

1. In your journal, write answers to these questions:

    a. Who are you?
    b. Where do you come from?
    c. Why are you here?

2. How did you acquire these beliefs?

Next, I will look at the topic of spiritual beliefs. If you are like most people, your spiritual beliefs come from two prevailing worldviews: materialism and religion. Although a comprehensive critique of these worldviews is beyond the scope of this book, I will briefly examine their limitations, since doing so is a necessary step toward adopting a new, empowered worldview.

Materialism

Science is stunningly precise in describing material phenomena. When it attempts to apply this narrow material knowledge to consciousness, however, it runs into what is termed "The Hard Problem."

Broadly put, metaphysical materialism posits that reality is composed of a set of subatomic particles. These particles are the building blocks of nature and account for the existence of everything—from a rock to the human body and mind, and out to the entirety of the Milky Way. Materialism further assumes that these subatomic particles are without consciousness and are therefore "dead." Now, here is the baffling question: *How can you get consciousness simply by arranging "dead" matter together?* There you have it: the hard problem of consciousness.

The worldview of materialism does not have an answer to the hard problem, but it maintains that consciousness *somehow* arises from matter and is confined to the brain. In other words: *the brain creates consciousness.* In this model, the brain is, in effect, a computer that runs the program we know as consciousness; thus, consciousness ceases to exist when the brain stops functioning. Materialism views life as essentially meaningless, because it proposes that life arises from random chance as a play of particles and is destroyed at death.

The core problem with materialism is its inability to explain even the basic phenomena of consciousness. Consider the cases of people who undergo brief clinical death, a phenomenon that has become more frequent with advances in medicine. In some cases, as observed by EEG machines, the electrical activity in their brains ceases completely. Materialism predicts that, without brain activity, there would be no consciousness and thus no experience. Upon revival, however, some patients narrate transformative experiences collectively known as "near-death experiences." The sheer number of such experiences, in millions according to some estimates, underscores that matter is not the source of consciousness and therefore that materialism is not the correct model of reality.

Furthermore, the foundation of materialism has been challenged from within science itself. After the development of quantum mechanics in the early twentieth century, the notion of matter being the fundamental building block of reality came into question. Quantum mechanics postulates that matter is a manifestation of a deeper underlying reality—what's called the "quantum field." Many scientists argue that the universe can be better explained as having originated from consciousness, rather than from matter. I will return to the implications of quantum physics later in this chapter, but for now let me turn to the other major worldview—religion.

Religion

In contrast to materialism, religious worldviews offer *some* ideas about consciousness and its purpose, yet the ideas differ so drastically across the astonishing number of more than four thousand existing faiths that they fail to offer a coherent model of reality. Further, religion suffers from a fundamental limitation: since evidence-based inquiry is not a part of religion, no methods actually exist for validating these ideas and claims. Followers must accept ideas on *faith*—a core limitation. History is rife with examples of faith degenerating into superstition, and worse, into fundamentalism.

In the absence of methods, fundamentalism has played a major role in religion's expansion. Historically, when two religions with incompatible beliefs came into contact, the one that prevailed typically did so not because it offered a sounder philosophical foundation or more effective methods, but rather because its brute fundamentalism overpowered the other, gaining its believers largely through manipulation and force.

It is important to understand that religions did not always exist in the institutionalized form we see today. Before institutionalization, spirituality was about the gentle nurturing of one's connection to the world, not blindly following a prescription for salvation. For instance, the ancient Eastern concept of *dharma* (a Sanskrit word that translates to "a way of life") has nothing to do with believing in a religious doctrine. About two thousand years ago, however, this gentle approach was discarded with the rise of modern religion. Many religions that started with the mystical insight of an individual were later taken over by the ideology of *exclusive salvation*, which proposes that only one path leads to salvation.

The doctrine of exclusive salvation is toxic because it divides humanity into believers and nonbelievers. Believers see nonbelievers as flawed and consider it their *holy duty* to convert them using any means—ideological, economic, or physical coercion, sometimes even torture. If we look at the dark history of religious conversions, the conversions of rulers were often followed by the compulsory conversion of their subjects, resulting in genocide and ethnic cleansing of whole nations, such as that of the Old Prussians (a Baltic ethnicity that resisted Christianity between the tenth and thirteenth centuries).

Central to religion's expansion is its institutionalized power. Through association with the state, religions garnered tremendous power, which was then used to further its leaders' own interests rather than serving humanity. In the past few hundred years, the power of religion has been somewhat weakened due to the rise of science, global connectedness, and democracy, where fundamental rights are theoretically protected despite one's religious beliefs. Yet, religion remains a dominant force on our planet. Religions based on "exclusive salvation" continue to sow division, which in turn leads to conflict, terrorism, and war.

A Better Worldview: Evidence-Based Spirituality

Since materialism and religion are both inadequate as spiritual worldviews, we need an alternative. I believe that a new worldview, which I call the *evolutionary model of consciousness*, can be constructed based on widely researched phenomena of consciousness. I believe, furthermore, that such a worldview can serve as an evidence-based model that evolves with time, similar to science.

Here are the axioms of this model:

1. A human being is not the body-mind, but instead a consciousness that is experiencing the body-mind. The term *simulation hypothesis* is used for consciousness experiencing the virtual reality of physical existence.

2. Consciousness is neither destroyed nor judged at death; it instead transitions to a different dimension—what we may call the Source Dimension. Transition of consciousness is nothing unusual; we experience it *every day* when we transition from the dream state to the waking state. We perceive the dream as *real* during the dream state, but realize it wasn't real when we wake up. Upon death, consciousness transitions from a simulated reality to Source Reality, similar to Neo waking up in the movie *The Matrix*.

3. The simulation's purpose is to evolve consciousness. Just as a flight simulator is used to become a better pilot, human reality is a simulation to help consciousness evolve.

Understanding Consciousness: Exploring Death and Reincarnation

During the past half century or so, consciousness researchers have made tremendous efforts to probe the nature of reality. Their findings, scattered across multiple disciplines, can serve as puzzle pieces for assembling a working model.

Central to the evolutionary model of consciousness is the observation that consciousness has *an independent reality beyond the body-mind,* which means it exists before birth and beyond death. The periods marked by birth and death serve as chapters in a whole composed of many lifetimes. This phenomenon, called reincarnation, proposes that each of us is an indestructible unit of consciousness. We therefore need not fear death, nor the punitive God that some religions propose.

If the concept of reincarnation is new to you, or if you are deeply conditioned by materialism, it may be tempting to dismiss reincarnation as a fantasy. But overwhelming evidence from multiple disciplines suggests that there is more to this phenomenon than mere imagination: these disciplines include children's memories of past lives, near-death experiences, out-of-body experiences, past-life regressions, mystical experience, channeled material, and many others. These diverse sources of evidence—spanning cultures, time periods, and scientific fields—invite us to reconsider our beliefs about reality.

It is worth noting that the pioneers of reincarnation research, mostly M.D.s and Ph.D.s, are credible professionals. Furthermore, they were not raised with a belief in reincarnation but rather adopted it only after serious investigation and deliberation.

A comprehensive review of reincarnation research is beyond the scope of this book. Let's look, however, at a case study from the most thorough research in the field, pioneered by Dr. Ian Stevenson and Dr. Jim B. Tucker.

Stevenson was a Canadian-born American psychiatrist who was named Chair of Psychiatry at the University of Virginia at only 38 years old. He was enjoying a successful mainstream academic career when he read reports of young children who said that they remembered their past lives. Intrigued, he decided to investigate. In 1961, he visited India for a month and immediately found 25 cases that could not be explained as mere coincidences or fantasies. He also found similar cases in Sri Lanka.

Stevenson realized that this phenomenon was much more common than anyone suspected in the West. Over the next four decades, he undertook meticulous research into children's memories of previous lives, aiming to discover whether their statements could be verified. Tucker took over the research when Stevenson retired in 2002.

While most instances of children with past-life memories occur in cultures with a general belief in reincarnation, instances also occur in countries where no such influences exist, such as in the well-documented case of James Leininger.

At just two years old, James, born an American, visited an aviation museum with his father. The visit triggered a series of bewildering events that profoundly affected his family. James' father noted that upon seeing some World War II aircraft, the child James grew quiet. Then he began speaking about an "airplane on fire" and later experienced nightmares. He went on to describe dying when the Japanese shot down his plane. What surprised his father was that he gave specific details that included:

- the type of aircraft he was flying (a Corsair)
- the name of its American aircraft carrier (the USS *Natoma Bay*)
- the first and last name of a friend on the ship with him ("Jack Larsen")

- his previous incarnation's first name (also "James")
- the location of the crash (the Japanese island of Iwo Jima), and other specifics about it

Tucker became aware of the case after the parents eventually wrote a book about their journey to believing in reincarnation. He investigated their claims and found numerous pieces of contemporary, corroborating evidence, such as drawings by young James himself and notes and records that the family had retained. Further, a person was later identified as a pilot matching the child's statements: James Huston Jr., a pilot from the USS *Natoma Bay*, who was killed during the Iwo Jima operation. His plane was shot down in a strike against transport vessels in a harbor on the nearby island of Chichijima.

As part of his scientific research into the case, Tucker considered many alternative explanations. There was the possibility that the family was committing fraud, but that seemed unlikely. It was true that they had written a book and might have hoped to profit from it, yet the book was not published until James was twelve, meaning they would have to plan the fraud a decade in advance—a lot of work for little financial gain.

Could childhood fantasy be the answer? Tucker concluded that it seemed impossible that a child could make up such accurate facts. The child also of course had no access to research material, nor could he even have studied articles about the crash at just two years old.

Accepting the fact, then, that young James could not have gained knowledge about pilot Huston's life through normal means, the question became: could he have gained it by paranormal means? Was he psychic? When Tucker questioned them about any other unusual abilities James might possess, his parents said there were none. He was just an unexceptional, normal child in all ways, except for his past-life memories.

Based on the large amount of documentation in James' case and the process of elimination, Tucker concluded that the most likely reason for the connection James Leininger shared with James Huston Jr. was that Leininger had lived Huston's life before his current one.

Another indicator of past lives is the ability to understand a language to which one has no prior exposure, a phenomenon known by the term *xenoglossy*. On November 10, 1930, the *New York Evening Post* reported the case of Marie Skotnicki, a four-year-old girl from Warsaw, Poland. Although her parents spoke only Polish, Marie developed a habit of talking to herself in a foreign tongue no one understood; it was later determined to be pure *Gaelic*, a language she had never learned or even heard before.

I could go on and on with examples from the reincarnation research literature, such as those of James Leininger and Marie Skotnicki. These and many other such cases certainly strike me as overwhelming evidence in favor of reincarnation. That said, reincarnation cannot be proved in a way a mathematical theorem can be proved, which explains why the mainstream scientific community remains resistant to it. Yet they offer no alternate models to explain the widely researched phenomenon of consciousness.

Why Are You Here?

The study of reincarnation raises a fundamental question: *What is its purpose?*

Past-life regression therapy, a discipline of hypnotherapy, offers an answer. Regression therapy is used to uncover sources of psychological problems, such as phobias. Such problems are often caused by childhood trauma, which can be revealed during the course of therapy. But in the 1960s, multiple researchers discovered that their regressed patients had experienced their trauma in a *previous* lifetime. As past-life regression therapy evolved, therapists learned how to gain information about their patients' time between incarnations. This research came to have a specialized subfield, called *pre-birth planning*, which reveals that lifetimes are carefully planned to maximize growth from each incarnation. (I will discuss pre-birth planning in Step 4.)

The purpose of reincarnation—in fact, the purpose of existence itself—is *evolution of consciousness*. Each incarnation is an opportunity to learn how to make better choices and manifest higher consciousness.

A significant breakthrough in understanding spiritual evolution came from research by Dr. David Hawkins, an internationally renowned psychiatrist, researcher, and lecturer, who wrote the book *Power vs. Force*. Using applied kinesiology, a methodology of studying muscle strength, Dr. Hawkins calibrated the following map of consciousness and created a logarithmic scale for its stages of evolution:

Level	Log
Enlightenment	700-1,000
Peace	600
Joy	540
Love	500
Reason	400
Acceptance	350
Willingness	310
Neutrality	250
Courage	200
Pride	175
Anger	150
Desire	125
Fear	100
Grief	75
Apathy	50
Guilt	30
Shame	20

We will dive deeper into the consciousness map in Step 2, but for now I'll just highlight a few of its key insights.

Low states of consciousness resist the flow of life. For example, **shame**—the lowest state noted on the scale—may cause people to commit suicide, which is a rejection of life. The scale then goes up and reaches a pivotal level at 200, where consciousness begins to embrace life with **courage**.

Higher states of consciousness make the human journey one of joy, purpose, and contribution. The highest level of the scale is **enlightenment**, which is our eventual goal on the human journey.

A key insight presented by Dr. Hawkins is that, on average, people increase their consciousness *only by about five points per incarnation.* This means that to reach the state of **love** at level 500, they would need about a hundred incarnations. An effective spiritual path, however, can dramatically accelerate one's evolution and cut down the number of incarnations needed to "graduate" from the Earth School.

Where Do You Come From? — Exploring Non-duality

We have looked at the first and second fundamental questions of spirituality—*Who am I?* and *Why am I here?* Let's now examine the third fundamental question: Where does consciousness come from?

The answer can be found in the concept of non-duality (or oneness), which proposes:

Consciousness is ultimately a unified whole, and all apparent separations—between self and others, physical and non-physical, and, most significantly, between the Source of consciousness (*Brahman*) and individual self (*Atman*)—are illusions.

As the mystic Rumi beautifully said: "You are not a drop in the ocean. You are the ocean in a drop."

Non-duality proposes that there is a primal field of consciousness—call it *Source* or *Brahman*—that splits and becomes the infinite forms of individual consciousnesses. It becomes everything that appears to have a separate existence—rocks and trees, animals and people, and, most importantly, *you!*

At first glance, non-duality might seem shocking, because it contradicts ordinary experience: You experience yourself as obviously separate from your neighbor. More pertinent to our exploration, though, is that it attacks the very foundation of religion: How can there be "salvation" if there is no separation between Creator and created *to begin with?* After all, a drop needs no religion to merge into the ocean—*its own expanded self.*

For people with worldviews founded on duality, the concept of non-duality seems like heresy, just as the idea of the earth's revolving around the sun was once heretical. If you study enlightened beings, however, you will observe "oneness" as the transcending essence that unites them across time, culture, and tradition. Think about it—what does the statement of Jesus that "I and my father are one" *really* mean?

The spiritual, philosophical, scientific, and moral arguments for non-duality can fill entire libraries of books. For our exploration, however, we don't need elaborate arguments. If you feel that you are a spiritual person, you might already resonate with the idea of life's *interconnectedness*. Non-duality is just a step further—it invites us to consider that life is not merely interconnected; *life is one.*

In the rest of this chapter, we will examine the key concepts of non-duality.

Central to understanding non-duality is the recognition that things that *appear* separate are not really so; they instead are different manifestations of the same underlying reality.

The way to understand this is to distinguish substance from form. For instance, jewelry, coins, statues, and many other things can all be made from gold. These forms depend on the substance of gold, which has a physical reality independent of form. By studying gold's properties (through chemistry and physics, for example), rather than its forms, one understands a deeper reality.

Another way to understand non-duality is to examine energy. Electricity, for instance, manifests as *motion* in a fan, *light* in a light bulb, and *sound* in a speaker. In a computer, it manifests as an *intelligence* that can perform complex tasks.

Similarly, all forms in the universe are manifestations of the one underlying energy.

The Historic Origins of Non-duality

The concept of non-duality first appeared in ancient spiritual and philosophical texts in India, called the *Vedas*. During that time, spiritual attainment was so highly valued that half of one's life was dedicated to its pursuit: the first quarter devoted to study, the next quarter to household and worldly duties, and the remainder to spiritual progress. Over many generations, these concerted efforts produced an extensive philosophical and spiritual body of knowledge.

The Vedic texts form an elaborate treatise on the nature of reality and methods of spiritual attainment. At the end of the Vedic period (approximately 600 BCE), the distilled essence of the philosophical work led to books called the *Upanishads*, which are considered parts of Vedanta (meaning the "culmination of Vedas").

The Chhandogya Upanishad, which scholars estimate to be approximately 2,600 years old, is among those texts that explore non-duality in detail. In chapter 6 of that Upanishad, a dialogue occurs between the sage Uddalak and his son Shwetaketu. When Shwetaketu was 12 years old, his father sent him away for higher studies (akin to attending college in our day). When Shwetaketu returned after 12 years, he was so full of pride that Uddalak became concerned with his son's arrogance. Being the wise sage he was, Uddalak asked Shwetaketu if he had learned in his studies about what gives us the power to perceive. What, he asked, is the power through which the unknown becomes known?

This simple question humbled Shwetaketu. Although he had learned about medicine, mathematics, and even rules of proper conduct, he had not learned about the nature of reality. So, he requested his father to teach him. Uddalak then discussed with his son how form arises from substance and how manifestation comes from an underlying consciousness:

"Just as, my dear, by one copper ornament everything made of copper may be known—the modification is merely a verbal distinction, a name; the reality is just 'copper.'"

In other words, all forms are manifestations of one reality.

At the conclusion of his examination, Uddalak uttered the insightful words *Tat Twam Asi* ("Thou art That"). This famous phrase's meaning is that you are not merely a form of consciousness, but rather its root cause—its timeless and formless essence: Brahman (or Source). That you are separate from Source is merely an illusion.

Thou art That (Sanskrit: तत् त्वम् असि, *Chhandogya Upanishad 6.8.7 of the Sama Veda*) is called a Maha Vakya, or a supreme statement. All four Vedas have similar Maha Vakyas, such as:

- Inner Consciousness is Brahman (Sanskrit: प्रज्ञानं ब्रह्म) *Aitareya Upanishad 3.3 of the Rig Veda*)

- This Self is Brahman (Sanskrit: अयम् आत्मा ब्रह्म) *Mandukya Upanishad 1.2 of the Atharva Veda*)

- I am Brahman (Sanskrit: अहं ब्रह्मास्मि) *Brihadaranyaka Upanishad 1.4.10 of the Yajur Veda*)

In the millennia since the Vedic times, numerous sages have described the ultimate truth of oneness in many different ways. The clearest and most concise explanation was perhaps given by the sage Adi Shankara, who wrote a short poem called "Atma Shatakam," meaning "Six Verses for the Self." It reads (in my translation):

> I am not the mind, nor intellect, nor ego, nor senses. I am beyond.
>
> I am none of the triad of the observer, the process of observing, or the object being observed.
>
> I am all-pervasive. I am without attributes and without form.

I have attachment neither to the world, nor to liberation. I have no wishes for anything because I am everything, everywhere, every time, always in equilibrium.

I am, indeed, that Eternal Knowing and Bliss, that Love and Pure Consciousness, the Supreme Being.

The exploration of non-duality is not exclusive to Vedanta. In my opinion, the most profound exploration of non-duality is contained in the Ra material, a modern spiritual work that calls non-duality "The Law of One." Here is how Ra defines the Law of One:

> You are every thing, every being, every emotion, every event, every situation.
>
> You are unity.
>
> You are infinity.
>
> You are love/light, light/love.
>
> You are.
>
> This is the Law of One.

Non-duality and Mystical Experience

Compared to virtually every popular spiritual tradition today, non-duality offers a revolutionary model of reality. As seekers of transformation, however, we must not be satisfied merely with a model. We must instead ask the crucial question: Is non-duality merely a philosophy, or does it have any basis in practical experience?

It turns out that Vedanta, which predates religions, was not mere philosophy. It had three logical foundations and was closely aligned with the scientific method that was developed thousands of years later. The first foundation is *Shruti* (collective wisdom); this corresponds to teachings and books. The second is *Yukti* (reason). The third, and most important, is *Anubhav* (experience).

The sages who proclaimed their oneness with Source did so not because they wanted to propagate a doctrine but rather because they experienced that oneness in the depth of meditation. Such experiences remain available to humans even today.

Direct personal experience of oneness is called *samadhi*, a transcendental state of consciousness experienced by enlightened beings. The experience of oneness is common among yogis, dating from the earliest known accounts to those living in the modern age. Among the dozens of biographies and autobiographies about such yogis, the most popular ones are *Autobiography of a Yogi*, by Paramahansa Yogananda (1946); *Play of Consciousness*, by Swami Muktananda (1974); and *Sadhguru—More Than a Life*, by Arundhathi Subramaniam (2010).

Here is how Yogananda described his experience:

> My sense of identity was no longer narrowly confined to a body, but embraced the circumambient atoms. People on distant streets seemed to be moving gently over my own remote periphery. The roots of plants and trees appeared through a dim transparency of the soil; I discerned the inward flow of their sap.
>
> The whole vicinity lay bare before me. My ordinary frontal vision was now changed to a vast spherical sight, simultaneously all-perceptive. Through the back of my head I saw men strolling far down Rai Ghat Road, and noticed also a white cow who was leisurely approaching. When she reached the space in front of the open ashram gate, I observed her with my two physical eyes. As she passed by, behind the brick wall, I saw her clearly still.
>
> All objects within my panoramic gaze trembled and vibrated like quick motion pictures. My body, Master's, the pillared courtyard, the furniture and floor, the trees and sunshine, occasionally became violently agitated, until all melted into a luminescent sea; even as sugar crystals, thrown into a glass of water, dissolve after being shaken. The unifying light alternated with materializations of form, the metamorphoses revealing the law of cause and effect in creation.

Over time, the inner technology of yoga was developed to make the transcendental experience of samadhi available to seekers. The word *Yoga* means the union of the individual self (which has forgotten its true nature during incarnation) with the Supreme Self.

Non-duality and Science

The greatest breakthrough in our understanding of reality has unfolded with the development of modern physics, which broke down the notions of duality that were so firmly set by Newtonian physics—perhaps the epitome of a dualistic model of reality.

The Newtonian worldview considers the universe to be a big, deterministic machine. In the Newtonian paradigm, objects move in space because of forces acting on them; they are separate from such forces and also from other objects. This paradigm assigns no importance to consciousness, because it sees matter as the foundation of reality, which somehow *creates* consciousness but is itself *independent* of it.

The Newtonian worldview began to fall apart in the twentieth century with the rise of the theories of relativity and quantum mechanics. Relativity breaks down the duality of matter and energy. Albert Einstein's famous equation, $E=mc^2$, states that *matter is energy*. More importantly, *time and space are fundamentally the same physical entity*, known as "space-time."

Our understanding took another revolutionary leap with the development of *quantum mechanics*, the field that studies fundamental particles such as electrons and photons. Early-twentieth-century physicists discovered the puzzling truth that these particles can exhibit both wave-like and particle-like behavior, depending on how they are observed. This challenges the classical notion of distinct, independent entities and points to a deeper, unified reality beyond binary distinctions. Further, the phenomenon known as *quantum entanglement* demonstrates that particles can become correlated in such a way that the state of one particle instantaneously influences the state of another, *regardless of the distance between them*. This suggests a profound interconnectedness at the heart of reality, echoing the non-dual idea that all things are fundamentally one.

Quantum mechanics also breaks down barriers between the observer and the observed: that is, the act of observation affects the system being observed. If the observer affects the observed, consciousness must be a primal cause, rather than an effect created by matter. Consciousness can bring a particle into existence from the unmanifested field of possibility, thus affecting the very fabric of reality.

Quantum field theory holds that reality can be seen as an interplay of fields, which give rise to particles. Delving more deeply into the nature of these fields, physicists have asked the vital question: *How many fundamental fields are there?* Although physics has not yet come up with a definitive answer, many physicists (including Einstein himself) believe that these different fields are manifestations of a core that underlies the "Field of Fields." The quantum field that is the primal cause from which everything else arises is called the "Source Field," "Zero Point Energy," or simply "the Field." In the language I have used before, this Field would correspond to Source.

In recent decades, significant research has been done to understand the Field and its relationship to consciousness. The Field is the energetic backdrop of all existence, connecting every part of the universe with everything else through non-local quantum effects. Most importantly, the Field responds to consciousness. For example, a series of studies done in the 1970s investigated whether large-group meditation could lower crime rates. The result was a homicide rate reduction relative to the baseline average rate of 21.2% over the four-year intervention period. Such a drop was possible when a sufficiently large group practicing an advanced program of Transcendental Meditation (TM) focused their intention together. According to Michael Dillbeck, the lead author of a journal article titled "Societal Violence and Collective Consciousness: Reduction of U.S. Homicide and Urban Violent Crime Rates," research suggests that a large group practicing TM together can affect the collective field of consciousness and thereby contribute to the lowering of crime.

If you are interested in learning more about experiments related to the Field, a good starting point is the book *The Field*, by Lynne McTaggart.

Non-duality and Ethics

One of the main arguments for religion is that it provides a foundation for ethical living. The proponents of this view argue that without religion, humans will act solely out of self-interest, and as a result our civilization will degenerate into a dog-eat-dog world.

In my view, however, non-duality provides a better foundation for ethics: We should treat our neighbors as ourselves because *they come from the same source as us* and thus are our spiritual siblings.

We love our siblings regardless of their spiritual beliefs. The true understanding of non-duality frees us from needing to impose our beliefs on others. Even if people don't understand anything about non-duality (and likely don't want to!), they are still our siblings and deserve the love reserved for our kin.

Ethics rooted in oneness transcends all human-made boundaries—religious dogma, cultural and national identity, and egocentric thinking—offering instead an inclusive, universal basis for ethical living. By embracing non-duality, we can create a world rooted in compassion, love, and harmony, where ethics is not merely a set of rules to follow but rather a natural expression of our oneness with all sentient beings.

Non-duality: From Oneness to Many-ness

I will conclude the discussion of non-duality by answering a puzzling philosophical question: Why does the ocean of consciousness (Source) become individual drops (individuated consciousnesses)?

According to non-duality, pure conscious energy lies at the core of existence. It is the *only* underlying reality; let's call it *Unity*. Since Unity is all that exists, paradoxically, it runs into a limitation: *It cannot have an experience*. To have an experience, it needs something outside itself to act as the object of that experience.

So, Unity splits itself into an infinite number of individual consciousnesses and becomes *Infinity*.

Since Unity is pure consciousness, each of its portions is also pure consciousness, but now each portion can perceive "otherness." This is you and me! This state of connected Infinity is the locus where a limitless number of consciousnesses exist and are aware of their oneness. Knowing that all existence is an extension of the Self, the Self can explore consciousness in infinite ways through its interaction with Infinity.

The state of existence within connected Infinity seems perfect but in truth is incomplete, because it excludes a core aspect of existence: *separation*.

Now, you may ask why any consciousness would choose to experience separation. The answer is that there are some types of learning that can only happen in the state of separation.

Consider power, for example. A significant portion of human existence is spent learning about various aspects of power—lack of power, thirst for power, and choices related to the use of power. In the state of connected Infinity, the concept of power cannot exist, because all consciousnesses know themselves as one. It is only by perceiving themselves as separate from others that people can play the game of power.

To experience separation, consciousness creates the shell of *ego*. (Please note that I use the word *ego* here as a spiritual term, referring to "the false self," rather than to the Freudian concept of ego.) The false self is created by identifying with what you are *not*. For example, you might think of yourself as a man or a woman and thus create an entire set of beliefs and restrictions based on that gender identification. In reality, you are neither a man *nor* a woman. You have a body that *comes with a gender*.

The "false self" hides the "true self," just like a blanket wrapped around a lightbulb hides the light.

For physical incarnation, there is yet another layer that the Self creates: personality. One's personality offers one unique ways to perceive and interact with existence. For example, having an adventurous personality enables one to explore freely. In contrast, a timid personality causes one to be calculative and cautious. Neither is better than the other, because each serves a unique purpose.

When many such Selves exist—all hidden under the structures of ego and personality, oblivious to their oneness with each other—they can play the "incarnation game." It is a game of infinite complexity, growth, and beauty.

Conclusion

Our quest for a better worldview began with the three core questions of human existence. We found the answers supported both by evidence of reincarnation and by the philosophical foundations of non-duality. Reincarnation provides the *mechanism*—the "what" of spirituality. Non-duality provides the framework for the *origin* of consciousness. And evolution of consciousness provides the *process*—the "how" of spirituality. Here is a summary:

— *Who are you?*
You are a consciousness exploring reality through human experience.

— *Where do you come from?*
You come from Source, and so does everything else. You are an individuated portion of Source Energy, and so are all beings.

— *Why are you here?*
The purpose of the human journey is the evolution of consciousness. Higher consciousness manifests states of peace, love, joy, and harmony. The ultimate aim of the human journey is enlightenment.

EXERCISE
Examine Your Beliefs

This chapter introduced a new belief system that, depending on your existing worldview, may appear radical. As I have underscored in this chapter, beliefs carry enormous power because they create reality. To gain greater insight into your beliefs, write down answers to the following questions in your journal:

1. On a scale of 1 (super-easy!) to 10 (impossible!), how difficult do you find it to believe in reincarnation and non-duality?

2. If your number is above 5, why do you find them so hard to believe?

3. Compared to materialism and religion, in what ways might reincarnation offer you a more empowering perspective on the human journey?

4. If you could see yourself and others as manifestations of Source Energy, how might that change your life?

GERRY'S JOURNEY

Where do you start the journey of spiritual transformation? How must your worldview change to make the journey possible? Gerry shows us that, through compassion and self-reflection, we can find our path.

My spiritual transformation began with the unraveling of my life in January of 2017. Within one week, my girlfriend left me, and I was in a severe car accident. As I lay in the emergency room with a broken collarbone, alone in a foreign country, I reflected on how I had hit rock bottom.

I had moved to Canada after earning a degree in music production in the U.K., and I was keen to find success in love and career. Perhaps more painful than the car that hit me was the realization that I'd failed to find success in either endeavor. I was lonely, miserable, and without purpose. The car accident forced me to face uncomfortable questions about life and who I was.

I was born in France. As a young boy, I remember sitting in my backyard and feeling in touch with an all-pervasive Presence. The experience felt as natural as basking in the sun, and I would stay in that state for hours. Although I did not know it then, that was my first experience of meditation and expanded consciousness.

At age eight, I was introduced to Catholicism. Jesus's example of compassion made a deep impression on my young mind. I yearned for a deeper understanding of my Christian faith, and I strived to become more like Jesus. But by the time I reached age sixteen, multiple scandals in the Church came to the national limelight, and I lost faith in religion.

For the next two decades, I busied myself fulfilling the materialistic goals of getting a good education and having a successful career. Music stirred my soul, and I was excited to earn a degree in music production.

Although my life was going well externally, something was missing. I longed for a meaningful life but didn't know what that looked like. When I graduated from college in 2013, Britain was undergoing a recession and my dreams of making it big in the music industry shattered. I lifted myself from the depressing situation by reading books on success. I devoured books by Napoleon Hill. This helped, and my career moved slowly back on track.

In 2016, I moved to Canada to start a new life. The months after arriving in Canada were full of exciting new experiences. Once again, I felt I was finally going to live the life I had dreamed of.

Lying in that emergency room in Toronto, broken and alone, I finally realized what I was missing—the connection with Presence. No amount of outside success could fill that void.

Once out of the hospital, I decided to make major changes in my life. I knew if I was to go far in my spiritual endeavor, I mustn't go alone; I needed a community. I signed up for yoga, movement, and breathwork classes at my local YMCA. In that humble place, I discovered Kundalini Yoga, a practice that would become the cornerstone of my spiritual transformation.

I immediately gained a deep sense of peace through these practices. By mid-2017, however, something unexpected started to happen. While sitting in meditation, my body would automatically move and assume strange postures. I started seeing fractal patterns of light and color when I closed my eyes. At first, I felt scared. Was I possessed? But the experience of peace that inevitably followed was so deep, I dismissed that possibility. I searched online and found I was going through kundalini awakening.

By the second half of 2017, my day-to-day experience of life had transformed. I remember a day when I was waiting for a bus. There was nothing extraordinary about the day; however, everything around me seemed strangely alive. People seemed like actors, and life an enormous play.

These little episodes of connecting with Presence in my everyday life became more frequent, culminating in a life-transforming experience in December 2017.

I still remember the day and exactly how it happened. I woke up before my alarm, feeling refreshed and energized. I was lying on the couch listening to the music of Jordan Raquette when, suddenly, my consciousness expanded, and I started *witnessing* myself and my thoughts. It was as if I wasn't just a person experiencing things but also the experience and the presence enveloping the experience. Words are inadequate to describe how it felt. Although I continued to work and live as usual, my actions arose from a place of bliss, not from considerations of the past or future. This expanded state lasted for a week before ending as abruptly as it had begun.

Trying to understand this awakening led me to explore books about deeper aspects of consciousness and mystical experiences. I came across the works of David Hawkins and learned that I had undergone *samadhi*— an experience of oneness. What's fascinating to me is that there have been beings on our planet who lived in uninterrupted samadhi. An example is Ramana Maharshi, an Indian mystic who started the "Who Am I?" spiritual movement.

In 2019, I took a break from my freelance work to spend time near Maharshi's ashram in India. Every day, I would visit his ashram, where I experienced the same spiritual energy I had felt in Toronto, even though Maharshi had left his body seventy years before. In India, I connected with many spiritual teachers and seekers from all over the world, but the greatest gift I received was experiencing my Inner Knower (*Antaḥkaraṇa* in Sanskrit), the voice of inner guidance. The Knower guided me to return to Canada and pursue my spiritual path in the West.

Within a few months after I arrived back in Canada, there was a COVID lockdown. My search for community led me to Children of Infinity. Dr. Narayan's efforts to improve the practical aspect of human experience by focusing on core beliefs appealed to me. I was fortunate to take part in a year-long course where we read books about reincarnation and pre-birth planning. I realized that I am not alone on this human journey. The program helped me to let go of fear and self-criticism, and I finally summoned up the courage to chart my own path.

I am now training to be a meditation teacher, and I have found joy in working with beginners, in whom I see my younger self. To me, the spiritual journey begins with mindfulness, which is a keen awareness of one's beliefs, choices, and behaviors. I aspire to emulate my teachers and lead people to greater compassion and joy.

Gerry (Gerald) Trepy is an award-winning sound producer as well as a meditation teacher living in Toronto, Canada.

Step 2: Accelerate Your Spiritual Evolution

"The strongest and most vital of all the powers of nature is the power of change."

—Charles Darwin

"Do you not see how necessary a world of pains and troubles is to school an intelligence and make it a soul?"

—John Keats

In Step 1, I introduced the *evolutionary model* of spirituality, which proposes that each human being is an individuated consciousness that seeks richness of experience through incarnations. Learning through incarnations spans multiple lifetimes, akin to progressing through grades in a school.

Though spiritual evolution is a natural function of consciousness, in the absence of intentional effort, it happens rather slowly—at the rate of about five points per incarnation. Authentic spiritual tools, however, can help you bypass the slow lane of spiritual growth to get onto the fast lane of *spiritual revolution*. The fast lane enables you to graduate from the Earth school in a few incarnations, rather than hundreds.

In the subsequent chapters in this book, we will explore the tools and practices of spiritual revolution in depth, but first, I want to devote this chapter to exploring the journey of spiritual evolution.

The evolution of consciousness poses deep metaphysical questions:

- What are the stages of spiritual evolution?

- What was the nature of consciousness before it evolved into human form?

- What becomes of consciousness upon graduation from human experience?

Research conducted over the past 50 years can help us build a model to answer these questions. We will review such research under two categories: the macro view of evolution, which extends beyond human experience, and the micro view of evolution, which lies within human experience.

The Macro View: Evolution of Consciousness Beyond Human Experience

The macro view of evolution is concerned with all manifestations of consciousness, not only that of humans. We can observe that animals possess consciousness that appears *less evolved* than humans. Does it not then stand to reason that in an infinite Universe there must be forms of consciousness *more evolved* than humans?

In my 25-year study of metaphysics, I have found that the most comprehensive information about evolution of consciousness is contained in the Ra material (also known as the *Law of One* material), a set of channeled sessions conducted between 1981 and 1984.[1] (These sessions, available in audio and text, can be accessed for free on the L&L Research website: https://www.llresearch.org.)

According to Ra material, consciousness evolves through stages of reality called *densities*. The higher the density level, the more light—or strands of Source Energy—is available for learning and creation. Each higher density offers a more complex reality and higher evolutionary stages of consciousness.

An insightful example of the evolution of complexity is movies. The motion picture industry started in the late nineteenth century with simple black-and-white images moving so quickly they created an illusion of motion. They lacked an important element, though: sound. A revolutionary leap came in 1927 when sound was added to the motion picture *The Jazz Singer*. With this added dimension, movies became much more expressive. Since then, the art form has made significant advancements with the introduction of color, background score, special effects, and animation.

Just as greater complexity enables expressing greater creativity in movies, higher densities offer consciousness a richer framework to express the creative force of Source Energy.

An Introduction to Densities

According to the Ra material, the journey of consciousness begins at Source, the primal energetic cause of consciousness. From this field, individualized consciousness is born and embarks on a unique evolu-

---

[1] Channeling is a process where information from the non-physical dimension can be transmitted to the human realm. Channels have existed throughout human history. Modern channels include Daryl Anka, who channels Bashar, an evolved consciousness, and Lee Carroll, who channels Kryon.

tionary journey. Ra proposes that there are seven densities that form the basis for evolution of consciousness. Similar to notes on a musical scale, the seven densities form a single octave within a larger cycle of evolution. The octaves then repeat indefinitely, rendering existence infinite.

Let's briefly explore the seven densities and the evolutionary opportunities they offer.

- The beginning stage of this journey is the **first density**. This is the <u>density of existence</u> in its most primitive form: *matter*. Basic elemental forms, such as rocks, sand, and water, are examples of first density. While a rock may not seem conscious to us, its constituent substance—matter—is itself a form of intelligent energy. Matter forms the basis of life and supports the creation of higher densities. At this stage of existence, consciousness inhabits an *atomic* body.

- In the **second density**, consciousness experiences movement and growth. This is the density of <u>animal and plant life,</u> ranging from unicellular organisms to complex animals. The second-density form inhabits a *chemical* body that requires sustenance and is subject to decay based on physical laws.

- The **third density** is the one in which we, as human beings, are currently evolving. This is the <u>density of self-awareness and free will.</u> These two faculties enable consciousness to *choose* how it interacts with other beings. Unsurprisingly, this density is also referred to as the density of choice.

  Within this density, one must make a metaphysical choice between service to oneself or service to others—two opposing options that represent a polarity of consciousness. To graduate from this density, one must commit sufficiently to one of the two options. (I will delve more into the third density after briefly discussing the higher densities.)

A human trying to grasp densities higher than the third is a bit like the aforementioned rock trying to understand a cat, or a cat trying to understand human civilization. Numerous conceptual and linguistic limitations make this exploration challenging, but we will do the best we can within the confines of language.

- Upon graduation from the third density, consciousness ascends to the **fourth density**, the <u>density of love.</u> Several fundamental changes occur. As part of its evolution, consciousness learns collective cooperation in addition to individual expression. This is similar to how unicellular organisms combine to form complex plants and animals: imagine if all of humanity could operate as one unified consciousness instead of separate beings. The other change is that the body advances from a chemical vessel for consciousness to a light vessel. The light body does not suffer from the physical limitations that affect the chemical body.

- The **fifth density**, known as the <u>density of wisdom,</u> is about learning to balance love with wisdom. While love is a powerful force, it cannot be used for the greatest good without adequate wisdom. The density of wisdom is about learning how to best harness the power of love to serve creation.

- The **sixth density** is the <u>density of unity and balance.</u> The goal in this density is to achieve the perfect balance between love and light—elements that are separately mastered in the fourth and fifth densities.

- The **seventh density**, called the <u>gateway density</u>, is the highest in an octave of evolution. At this stage, the individual consciousness is ready to merge itself back into the originating Source. In this density, the separation between Source and individual consciousness dissolves, enabling consciousness to recognize itself as Source and experience eternity.

The journey through the seven densities creates a grand spiral of evolution at the universal scale: a magnificent adventure of exploring and mastering the creative force of Source Energy. Once the entire octave of evolution has been experienced, the universe renews itself to commence subsequent octaves. Incidentally, the famous scientist Stephen Hawking promoted a cyclical theory of the universe in which the universe begins, expands, and then collapses into a formless vacuum that spawns new universes.

How to Graduate from the Third Density

What lessons do you need to master in order to graduate from humanity's current density of choice?

According to the Ra material, there are two pathways to graduation: (1) service to others (the positive path) or (2) service to oneself (the negative path). While both paths facilitate evolution and lead ultimately to Source, experiences on them differ. The path of service to others is the path of achieving harmony as a society, while the path of service to self is that of gaining power over others. The negative path is the path of power struggle, which leads to disharmony and suffering, and is thus the more difficult of the two paths.

Here, I will focus on the path of service to others. On this path, instead of putting self-interest above the interest of others, one makes choices that contribute to the collective well-being. Service to others requires evolving beyond the deeply ingrained instincts of survival and competition, which are inherent in the second-density animal experience. To be an evolved human is to rise above animal instincts and think of collective well-being. Only by putting cooperation above competition can a human progress to higher consciousness.

On the path of service to others, a common concern is balance. How can you concentrate on serving others without overlooking your own needs?

Importantly, serving others does not imply that all your actions must solely benefit the collective while disregarding your own needs. These two choices are not mutually exclusive. The Ra material suggests that you balance concern for others equally with concern for yourself. Your choices should aim to benefit both yourself and others without neglecting either party.

The key is service, *not* sacrifice. Some spiritual traditions heavily emphasize sacrifice, but this is an unwise approach. Spiritual maturity requires that you honor yourself with self-care, rejuvenation, joyous activities, and pleasure—while also honoring others. Only by caring for yourself can you serve with joy instead of obligation.

When you are guided by wisdom, your actions benefit others as well as you. When you plant flowers for a neighbor, you too will benefit from their beauty and fragrance. Genuine concern for others enables you to experience the joy of service, which originates from the primal frequency of love.

The Micro View: Evolution of Consciousness Within Human Experience

The micro view of evolution concerns evolution within human experience. While we intuitively understand that people manifest vastly differing levels of consciousness (think of Hitler compared to Gandhi), is it possible to quantify these? Yes. As mentioned in Step 1, Dr. David Hawkins applied kinesiology to calibrate levels of human consciousness, which he compiled in the map below.

Level	Log
Enlightenment	700-1000
Peace	600
Joy	540
Love	500
Reason	400
Acceptance	350
Willingness	310
Neutrality	250
Courage	200
Pride	175
Anger	150
Desire	125
Fear	100
Grief	75
Apathy	50
Guilt	30
Shame	20

Here are the seven key insights from Dr. Hawkins's pioneering research:

1. The numbers on the map correspond to spiritual power. The higher the number, the higher one's state of evolution and, consequently, the higher one's ability to do spiritual work, which is to manifest love.

2. The states of consciousness are divided into three broad categories:

    a. *Consciousness opposing life (below 200).* These stages oppose existence and create suffering. Lower states, such as **shame,** reject the gift of life and may result in suicide. The highest scale below 200, **pride,** refuses life by adopting ideologies such as nationalism or religion—ideologies rife with seeds of conflict, violence, and war that deny life to those who disagree with the ideology.

    b. *Consciousness supporting life (200-500).* In these stages, one begins to rejoice in the gift of life and express internal power, which allows one to see oneself as the creator rather than the victim of one's experience. At this stage, life begins to align with meaning, purpose, and well-being.

    c. *Transformative consciousness (500-1000).* These stages, the highest possible on the human journey, exert tremendous spiritual power and can inspire and transform entire populations. People such as Gandhi, Mother Teresa, and Martin Luther King Jr. fall into this category. Their examples influence generations of humans and change the fabric of society.

3. The scale is logarithmic, meaning the power increases exponentially with a rise in consciousness. A single individual at level 700 can counterbalance 70 million individuals below level 200.

4. Similar to individual consciousness, Dr. Hawkins calibrated the collective consciousness of humanity. The collective human consciousness stayed below the 200 level (190) for many centuries before it finally broke through the 200 level sometime in the mid-1980s. However, 85% of the human race still calibrates below the critical level of 200.

5. Everything calibrates at certain levels—not just people but also books, food, water, clothes, animals, buildings, cars, movies, sports, music, etc. Most of what is mass-produced today, including processed foods and entertainment (music, TV, and movies), calibrates below the level of 200. Thus, it is essential for those who wish to evolve above 200 to undertake diet and media detoxes.

6. Higher states of consciousness are exceedingly rare. Only 0.4% of the world's population ever reaches the level of **love** at 500.

7. There is a straightforward practice for raising your consciousness:

   a. Avoid everything below level 200. This insight is the basis of the next step in this book: detoxing. Pay attention to how influences in the world make you feel. A level below 200 arouses feelings of **inadequacy, fear, anger,** and **pride.**

b. Actively associate with people, teachings, and sacred symbols that calibrate at 500 or above. Since 500 is the level of **love,** these associations create a sense of inspiration and love for yourself, your fellow beings, and all of existence.

A Brief Overview of Stages on the Map of Consciousness

The map of consciousness is an essential tool in spiritual growth because it reflects where you are on your journey. The levels are titled with words that describe a universal emotion, but remember that, in this context, they refer to stages of consciousness. Let's briefly review the research by Dr. Hawkins:

Shame: (20)
Shame causes you to view your entire self in a negative light. It makes you want to sink into the ground or become invisible. It is destructive to emotional and mental health and makes you more likely to suffer physical illness. The level of shame referenced here is close to death. It may result in life-shortening behaviors, such as drug or alcohol abuse, or even suicide.

Guilt: (30)
Guilt is the cousin of shame. You may experience guilt by feeling remorse, self-recrimination, or masochism. Unconscious guilt results in psychosomatic illnesses such as hypertension, respiratory ailments, gastrointestinal disturbances, migraine headaches, sexual dysfunction, or dermatitis. Guilt also provokes inner anger, which may result in violence.

Apathy: (50)
Apathy is a state of helplessness characterized by a lack of response to something that normally elicits excitement in you. Despair, hopelessness, and poverty characterize this level. One's existence and future seem bleak. But don't be mistaken: the main issue isn't a lack of resources but a lack of energy to make the best of what's available. People at this level may still contemplate death by suicide.

Grief: (75)
No doubt you will experience grief at some point in your life. Everyone does, but normal grief passes organically. Those who live mainly at this level endure a life of constant mourning and regret about the past. Similar to the levels below it, grief has negative physical, cognitive, and behavioral consequences. In grief, you see and experience sadness, loss, and dependency everywhere you look. This level shrouds your entire existence in darkness.

Fear: (100)
Fear has been common throughout history, and it is still the common stage of mass consciousness. For those at this level, the world appears dangerous. If fear is your focus, there are plenty of issues—both real and imagined—to help it grow. Fears of war, crime, and illness are all rational. However, today's media profits from deliberately broadcasting a steady diet of bloody stories to keep you in a state of fear. Fear quickly becomes obsessive; it limits your personality's growth and leads to a reluctance to seek new experiences. Living at the level of fear, you are oppressed and lack energy, unable to reach higher states.

Desire: (125)
While desire may drive you to put in considerable effort to achieve

your goals, the issue at this level is that you may not be seeking the right goals. Desire is associated with consumption, greed, and the accumulation of assets. Like lower levels that can lead to drug and alcohol abuse, those at the level of desire are prone to addiction. Forms of desire, such as the desire for profit—over protecting the environment—can become cravings greater than respect for life. However, because it is goal-driven, desire can also be a springboard to begin the journey to higher levels of consciousness.

Anger: (150)
Anger stems from the energy field below it, as desire leads to wanting—and if you do not get what you want, frustration follows. This level is expressed through resentment and revenge-seeking. Anger is volatile and can lead to violent and dangerous actions. It feeds hate, and there are tragic consequences when hate fills all areas of a person's life.

Pride: (175)
Pride is a conflicting level. While you may feel positive when you reach this point, pride is dependent upon forms of external validation. If those validating conditions aren't met, you can return to a lower level. Pride operates on an inflated ego, which produces arrogance and denial and hinders inner growth.

Courage: (200)
The level of courage is the transition point from the levels below it, where the world appears hopeless, sad, frightening, and dangerous. At this new level, things begin to improve because authentic power becomes available. The world becomes exciting and stimulating. It is a place for exploration and achievement. With empowerment and determination, you can effectively manage life's opportunities. Therefore, the goals of educating yourself and growing spiritually

become desirable and attainable. Challenges in life, which may discourage those with a consciousness level below 200, serve as motivators for individuals who have attained this initial stage of genuine power.

Neutrality: (250)

Once you reach this level, your energy begins to operate positively. Neutrality promotes flexibility and a realistic evaluation of challenges. Rather than aiming to get your own way at all costs, neutrality strives for mutually beneficial outcomes. With little interest in being judgmental, controlling, or involved in conflict, you will be comfortable with yourself and emotionally stable. Naturally, people at this level are easy to get along with and safe to associate with.

Willingness: (310)

This is a gateway to higher consciousness. At the level of willingness, growth becomes rapid. You work well, enjoy success in your endeavors, and continue to advance. As you achieve social and economic success, you naturally experience a desire to share it with others and make a positive contribution to society. You are also willing to look internally, solve problems, bounce back from adversity, and learn from experience.

Acceptance: (350)

This level is about transformation. You finally understand you are the source and creator of your life experiences. Previously, you saw your problems as "out there." Now, you accept that nothing external can bring happiness. Love can never be given or taken away by another person—it comes from within yourself. You become the master of your life.

Reason: (400)

Rational intellect takes precedence over emotions at this level. This is the level of science and an increased capacity for knowledge, education, and understanding. Einstein, Freud, Jung, and other great thinkers in history belong here. Limits remain, though, as reason does not provide a complete path to truth. Reason alone cannot help you to distinguish between symbols and what they represent. Reason can also pose a considerable obstacle to attaining higher levels of consciousness, which is why transcending this level is rare.

Love: (500)
The state of love explored here differs from the one depicted in mass media. Popular conceptions of love consider it just another commodity, and at a superficial, emotional level, when love is taken away, it turns into anger. The notion of love turning into hate is simply a misconception, as hate originates from pride. Hawkins's map of consciousness characterizes love as *a state of being* rather than an emotion. It is unconditional and everlasting because its source isn't dependent on external factors. This love focuses on the goodness of life. Only 0.4% of people reach this level of consciousness.

Joy: (540)
Joy comes from genuinely experiencing each moment of existence. When you attain this level, you can persist with patience and positivity in the face of adversity. Creation's beauty lights the world. You realize everything occurs through synchronicity, and you can experience phenomena outside conventional expectations of reality. Transformative events, such as near-death experiences, have frequently allowed people to experience this level's energy by removing the veil between the physical and non-physical. Inner joy is characteristic of advanced spiritual teachers and healers abiding at this level.

Peace: (600)
People who achieve this state sometimes report that life appears to be occurring in slow motion, suspended in time and space. All around you, the world is alive and radiant. This energy field radiates transcendence, self-realization, and consciousness. This is a revelation that can only take place in a non-rational way. The mind stops conceptualizing and becomes silent. Great works of art, music, and architecture are created here. The level of peace is scarce—achieved by only about 1 in 10 million people.

Enlightenment: (700-1000)
Enlightenment is a vast scale, expanding from 700 to 1000. At this level, the body becomes a tool of consciousness. There is no longer an identification with the physical body as "you." Finally, you reach non-duality, or complete oneness with others, the world, and the universal energy field. This is the peak of evolutionary consciousness in the human realm. Enlightenment is an awareness of the meaning of existence and a release of all pain and suffering. Throughout history, only a handful of spiritual leaders have achieved this level of consciousness.

Conclusion

Both the macro and micro models highlight the crucial role that love plays in accelerating spiritual evolution.

The very purpose of human existence is to learn how to love.

When love overflows from us, it transforms us and makes our existence a gift. The purpose of the spiritual path is to achieve love consciousness.

Here are the practical guidelines that arise from love consciousness:

honor yourself and *honor others*. These four simple words contain all the wisdom needed to master the human journey, and the rest of this book explores the tools and practices devoted to this end.

First, here are three ways to begin the core practice of honoring yourself:

Honor Yourself

1. **Let go of what does not serve you.** Relinquish toxic emotions such as guilt, shame, and unworthiness. These are burdens picked up from social or religious conditioning that inculcates *sin consciousness*—the idea that you were born flawed. Let go of anything else that imprisons you and makes your journey strenuous. Take the tale of the South Indian Monkey Trap from Robert M. Pirsig's book, *Zen and the Art of Motorcycle Maintenance:*

   > The trap consists of a hollowed-out coconut chained to a stake. The coconut has some rice inside which can be grabbed through a small hole. The hole is big enough so that the monkey's hand can go in, but too small for its fist with rice in it to come out. The monkey reaches in and is suddenly trapped—by nothing more than his own value rigidity. He can't revalue the rice. He cannot see that freedom without rice is more valuable than capture with it.

   This example is a reminder to let go of anything that prevents us from living our highest life.

2. **Have higher aspirations.** You bear the light of primal consciousness within. Honor this by living a life aligned with higher spiritual values rather than the meaningless pursuit of consumption and accumulation. There is more to life than

being a cog in the economic machinery. The universe is here to support you, but you must take the first step by seeking to live an inspired, fulfilled, and joyous life.

3. **Cultivate your gifts.** As a unique expression of Source Energy, you have gifts only you can offer to existence. So, use your resources—your time, attention, and money—to cultivate these gifts. Let go of meaningless activities such as social media, news, and passive entertainment. Invest that time in growth, which empowers you to uplift yourself and others.

From the perspective of non-duality, others are an extension of your being. We are all leaves on the tree of life—connected and supported by one source of consciousness. Here are two ways to honor this connection:

Honor Others

1. **See others as Source.** Each individual is on a unique journey to perfection, just as you are. When you honor others, you create peace and joy to share with the collective. Let go of the need to control or manipulate others. Treat them not with judgment but with compassion. Others may be very different from you and hold different opinions, but they are differing parts of yourself rather than separate adversaries.

2. **Serve.** Service is our highest calling as incarnate beings. When you serve without expecting anything in return, you manifest the highest level of consciousness. As a practical step, find at least one way to serve. Then, offer your service as a gift to existence.

Think about your skills and interests. If your skill is building or carpentry, perhaps there are less privileged communities in your town where you can help construct or refurbish buildings. If you feel compassion for animals, you could donate time to a shelter. If you are a teacher, are there children you can devote one-on-one time to help? Your example of service will inspire others and help them on their journey to higher consciousness.

Changing the world begins by changing yourself and your current environment. The first step to affecting grand change on a worldwide scale is to tidy up your room.

EXERCISE
Self-Inquiry to Honor Yourself and Others

Honoring yourself and others requires a conscious examination of your choices, small and big. Here is a short exercise to help you.

1. In your journal, list three ways to honor yourself. (For example, if you are in a job that does not fulfill you, you can honor yourself by trading it for more meaningful work.)

2. List three ways to honor those closest to you (e.g., family and friends).

3. List three ways you can honor humanity and all life on this planet.

SUZY'S JOURNEY

Spiritual journeys rarely follow a linear path. In fact, a spiritual transformation can often lead us back to where we started: childhood. Suzy shows us how trauma and conditioning can lead us away from our authentic selves and how meditation and other mindful practices can help us heal.

During a meditation in 2019, I saw myself walking down a narrow staircase, leading underground, where I eventually saw a dark, heavy door. Somewhere within me, I found the strength to open it. Inside was a sturdy, locked safe. I searched my mind, found the combination, and cracked the safe open. Inside it lay my heart, draped in thick, tightly wrapped cotton strips, like those used in paper mâché. This discovery made me realize why I couldn't receive love.

My mind wandered back to my childhood in St. Paul, Minnesota, to a time when I was a pre-pubescent 12-year-old girl pursuing my passions as an athlete and an artist with fervor. As I basked in this joyful memory, I realized my spirit had been trying to lead me back to this place of confidence and belonging, a time when my heart was open, and the world filled with possibilities.

My thirteenth year brought with it the transformation of puberty. Along with changes in my body, I found myself subscribing to the erroneous social construct that girls are only as valuable as the boys they can attract. I stopped following my passions and bent to the pressure of fitting in. I stopped following my inner guiding light and tried instead to attract the superficial limelight of attention.

However, my new-found popularity attracted trouble. For four months, I was tormented and humiliated by a group of girls. What started with notes left in my locker, and threatening phone calls, culminated in nearly a dozen girls cornering me and stealing my purse. I am still flabbergasted that these girls, who didn't really know me, hated me so much that they wanted to hurt me so badly. The police were called. I felt humiliated. The significance of this trauma in my life cannot be overstated. I was forced to close my heart and dim my light to not attract more attention.

In my twenties, I turned to alcohol and drugs to numb my pain. I dropped out of college and made one poor choice after another, including marrying someone totally incompatible. In 1988, he divorced me and left me as an impoverished single mother to a toddler. It was in those dire conditions that I finally resolved to build up the only person on whom I could rely—myself. I began my journey back to the 12-year-old girl in St. Paul, Minnesota, who understood joy and light.

I received a degree in teaching and began my tenure at a charter school in Minnesota in 1995. The charter was a place of peace and non-violence, a wonderful place for me to land. I held many positions there and was quite happy up until my seventh year of teaching, when my mother passed away.

As closed as my heart still was, nothing could have hurt it more than the pain of losing my mother, who was the only source of love in my life. I used the inheritance she left me to fund a year-long hiatus from teaching so I could heal. During that time, I spent a month in Jamaica working in a children's home. This mission of love and service did a great deal to mend my emotional wounds. But, as much as I longed to stay, I knew I needed to return to work. When I did, it felt as if my inner light had been completely put out. I spent the next several years being let go from various teaching positions for one reason or another. The struggle continued till 2014, nearly 11 years after my mother's passing. Finally, I embarked on what would be the best teaching years of my life. The administration trusted me, and I was allowed to do the work I was passionate about.

The opportunity for my transformation came in 2016 when, as part of a cohort at the University of Minnesota, I spent a year practicing mindfulness meditation. Deep inner work happened during that year. After finishing my training, I was given the opportunity to teach mindfulness to first graders as a specialist. This time of meditating, practicing yoga, and coloring with 6-year-olds went a long way to bring me back to myself.

Once I experienced the power of meditation, I started searching for a community. In 2021, shortly after retiring from teaching, I discovered Children of Infinity and began the work of opening my heart and returning to joyous living. I do not remember how I found this community. Perhaps it was a knowing, or I was ushered there by my spirit. I enrolled in a course on spiritual transformation that enabled me to work on the relationship between my body and soul. I have been using the "Stairway of Light" meditation daily for more than a year and have noticed deep changes in my underlying patterns. I can feel my soul making decisions and my body acquiescing. For example, after more than 40 years of drinking, I have become sober. Alcohol has become an allergen to my soul, something I can no longer stand.

Along with this life-changing transformation, I have finally been able to mend the heartbreak that plagued me for decades. I have not only become open to receiving love, but I am also offering unconditional love to people on the spiritual path as a leader within the Children of Infinity community. I have noticed that I am channeling divine energy and can feel the work being done through my humble vessel. I feel blessed to be of service as I continue my journey back to my authentic self.

Suzy Bergh is a community leader within Children of Infinity. She is a facilitator of the cohort program, "The Spiritual Transformation Quest."

Step 3: Detoxify and Disconnect

"All over the place, from the popular culture to the propaganda system, there is constant pressure to make people feel that they are helpless, that the only role they can have is to ratify decisions and to consume."

—Noam Chomsky

"Industrial societies turn their citizens into image-junkies; it is the most irresistible form of mental pollution."

—Susan Sontag

On the journey to wholeness, the first step is to detoxify—*to intentionally remove everything that hampers spiritual growth.* As mentioned in the last chapter, energetic influences below level 200 impede our development, similar to how toxic elements in soil hamper a plant's growth. This chapter provides the tools to detox the four major areas of your life: space, information, emotions, and relationships. Detoxing unblocks mental and spiritual energy, freeing it for spiritual evolution.

The Sources of Toxicity

Toxicity emerges from unhealthy patterns of thinking, feeling, and behaving. Through repetition and reinforcement, these patterns become deeply embedded and perpetuate disempowerment. If you're going to take a serious approach to detoxifying these patterns, you'll have to look not only at your thoughts, feelings, and behaviors but also at the toxic influences that are driving them.

One such influence, which has become globally pervasive, is consumerism—the relentless pursuit of buying and owning more possessions as a means of defining one's identity. When we evaluate the essential characteristics of consumerism on the map of consciousness, we find it promotes toxic states such as **fear** of inadequacy, **pride** of ownership, **shame** if we don't "own enough," and **anger** when we become frustrated in our pursuit of more.

To live in a consumer society is to live in a world of mass delusion. This delusion is propagated and normalized through the mass media. In the book *The Age of Missing Information* (2006), environmentalist and author Bill McKibben reflects on our society by examining twenty-four hours of programming from ninety-three cable stations, which were recorded and later analyzed. He reflects on the analysis:

> If you filter out all the messages that television sends us, if you boil the sap down into syrup—there's an underlying premise: *You are the most important thing on earth.* You, sitting there on the sofa, clutching the remote, are the heaviest object in the known universe. Around you must everything orbit. That seems like a very normal idea to us. We've been raised as good consumers, and consumers, above all, put their own interests first.

The machine of consumerism is designed to manufacture good consumers—*people who buy stuff they don't need with money they don't have to feel pleasures that don't last.* The machine is powered by the twin engines of marketing and mass production, each requiring an injection of toxicity into the mass consciousness to be effective.

Marketing has become an ever-present and all-powerful influence shaping our lives, cultivating the irresistible urge to buy whatever advertisers are selling. It presents one simple answer to all our problems: *Purchase a solution.* This toxic conditioning creates the delusion that solutions to our problems lie outside ourselves, not within. A logical correlate of this view is that we don't need inner work and growth; all we need is purchasing power. As professor Yuval Noah Harari writes in his book *Sapiens: A Brief History of Humankind* (2015):

> The supreme commandment of the rest of us is "Buy!" Most previous ethical systems presented people with a pretty tough deal. They were promised paradise, but only if they cultivated compassion and tolerance, overcame craving and anger, and restrained their selfish interests. This was too tough for most. The history of ethics is a sad tale of wonderful ideals that nobody can live up to…. The new ethic promises paradise on condition that the masses give free reign to their cravings and passions and buy more and more. This is the first religion in history whose followers actually do what they are asked to do. How though do we know that we'll really get paradise in return? We've seen it on television.

The second driving force of consumerism is mass production, which focuses on profits rather than well-being, and manufactures what sells rather than what's healthy. For example, industrial food production aims for long shelf life, low production cost, taste, and repeat business, which are all achieved by making food addictive. (Notice what's missing: nutrition.) Such food is mass produced using toxic chemicals and creates craving rather than satisfaction. That serves the industry perfectly well because craving is a quintessential gateway to profits. One example of a harmful chemical in food is monosodium glutamate (MSG), which makes food taste better but causes weight gain and metabolic syndromes. By consuming mass-produced food, we have become an unhealthy population.

Consumerism creates a prison that prevents true spiritual freedom. Most people are so caught up in the cycle of consumption, they have no time to cultivate the true gifts of human experience: self-knowledge, wisdom, inspired thinking and communication, and a higher vision of themselves as individuals, members of society, and children of the universe.

How to Remove Toxicity

The quest to grow a beautiful garden begins with pulling weeds and preparing the soil. Likewise, spiritual growth first requires creating a healthier and more supportive environment. It has two steps:

1. **Detox:** This step involves understanding how toxic influences work, then removing any accumulated toxins from your system.

    An important aspect of this step is to declutter physical items. Clutter impedes the natural flow of energy, thereby hindering growth; therefore, whatever does not serve must be removed.

2. **Disconnect:** Detoxing will have no lasting effects if you do not remove the *sources* of toxicity. Examine where the toxins in your life come from and eliminate those sources so the toxins will not build up again.

How To Detox the Four Major Areas of Your Life

You can begin the detox process by working on four major areas of your life: space, information, emotions, and relationships.

1. Space Detox

What does a messy room have to do with spiritual growth? Quite a lot, actually. Space acts as a physical conduit for spiritual energy. The ways in which a person's environment impacts their mind has been extensively studied and is well understood: the mind is naturally drawn to order, and constant visual reminders of disorder drain cognitive resources, increase anxiety levels, disturb sleep, and reduce the ability to focus.

To create order that will support you spiritually, declutter and energetically upgrade your environment using these five steps:

1. *Discard broken things.* Many people do not have a conscious process to remove what no longer works. As a result, they keep accumulating junk. The first step is to eliminate everything that is broken, unusable, or outmoded. If possible, donate them to people who can make use of the parts. Otherwise, recycle or discard them.

2. *Give away unused things.* This is harder than the first step because we tend to hold on to things we might use, as we tell ourselves... *someday.* In actuality, we never will. What have you not used in the last six months? Clothes? Shoes? Electronics? What about the boxes stored in your garage? If you haven't worn or used something in the past six months, chances are you never will. If the items are in working or wearable condition, donate them to charities or take them to recycling centers. While you may not need or use something, someone else may very well put it to good use.

3. *Clean and organize.* Vacuum, dust, wash, or wipe down your work and living environments until they become clean and inviting. Next, rearrange furniture and belongings in a way that makes it easy and quick to access what you need to carry out your regular tasks.

4. *Beautify.* Decorate and adorn your space with items that inspire you and bring beauty. This doesn't mean you need to spend heaps of money, or any for that matter. You can decorate your newly cleared space with plants, flowers, or pictures of loved ones. Don't overdo it. A functional and minimalist space will not only make it easier to carry out tasks but also to organize and maintain cleanliness.

5. *Disconnect from sources of clutter.* The only way to stop the stream of clutter is to guard against the entry of unneeded possessions. Avoid replacing items you have removed with new stuff. This step requires you to upgrade from the mindset of *consuming* to that of *conscious use.* To cultivate the discipline of disconnecting from clutter sources, stop discretionary consumption and, for the next 30 days, *buy only what you absolutely need,* such as food and other life essentials. Think carefully before you buy things. Do you really need this item, or is it merely a want? Is it vital for your well-being or just a nice-to-have? Is it a tool you need for growth? Is it an item you can use to de-stress or relax? Be ruthless. Stick to only what you truly need.

2. Information Detox

Spiritual growth requires attention—the ability to focus on higher objectives rather than socially conditioned ones. Unfortunately, our attention has been and is continuously being hijacked by consumerism. In order to keep large masses of humanity incessantly consuming goods and services, and to keep this unnatural thirst alive, an external agent is needed: marketing. The manipulative influence of marketing empowers advertisers to create an irresistible urge in people, transforming them into customers who purchase whatever is being sold. The most detrimental effect of this process is the exploitation of people's attention, which leads to distracted, unfulfilled living.

To understand the kind of economy we live in, let's look at two of the world's most valuable companies—Walmart and Facebook. In 2021, their market capitalization (which reflects how investors value publicly traded companies) was 400 billion and 500 billion dollars, respectively. (Yes, Facebook was worth more than Walmart.) If this valuation does not surprise you, consider this: if both Facebook and Walmart ceased operations tomorrow, what would be the consequences?

Millions of people would experience Facebook's disappearance as inconvenient; however, though you would no longer see feeds from your social network, you could still reach people in person, by phone, or email. I suspect that many people, within a few weeks, would come to feel relieved that Facebook was no longer taking up their time and attention. Walmart's closing, on the other hand, would create utter chaos because Walmart deals with goods that are indispensable to life: clothing, car products, health aids, home furnishings, electronics, hardware, pet supplies, and housewares.

Why, then, is Facebook one hundred billion dollars more valuable than Walmart? The answer lies in understanding their business models. Walmart is a retailer. Its customers—the general public—pay Walmart directly for their goods. Facebook, on the other hand, sells its users' attention to advertisers, who bid on it through ads. While Facebook may appear to be a convenient platform for staying connected with your social network, it is, in essence, a business that uses you. Its product is your attention, which fuels the engine of consumerism.

The attention economy started way before Facebook. In an insightful book, *The Attention Merchants* (2016), author Tim Wu traces the origins of attention mining back to 1830 when Benjamin Day, a shrewd businessman, upended the newspaper industry.

Before Day, newspapers functioned like any other commodity. The only people who paid for newspapers were those who could afford them. At the time, newspapers cost around 5 pence (equivalent to $2 in 2022) due to the high cost of production. Day realized he could profit by selling the *attention of his readers* to advertisers. He started selling his newspaper, the *New York Sun*, for a penny, way below the cost of production. His goal was to maximize the number of newspapers sold because the greater the number, the more advertisers would be willing to pay him.

In his quest to appeal to the masses, Day discovered something that is still part of the news industry's rulebook today: you can hook people's attention by presenting them with the worst side of humanity—the bizarre, lurid, grotesque, or shocking. ("If it bleeds, it leads.") Soon, the entire industry jumped on the bandwagon, leading to an uncontained spread of negativity. Most news networks today follow the same format, tirelessly showcasing what's wrong with humanity.

Day also found that selling fake but sensational news would keep readers hooked. For example, in 1835, the *Sun* ran a headline story about "astronomical discoveries" falsely attributed to the famous scientist Sir John Herschel. The five-part series described what Herschel allegedly witnessed on the moon, through his giant telescope—flying "man-bats" with insatiable libidos. The Sun even gave them a scientific-sounding name: Vespertilio-homo. The "moon-hoax" was instrumental in making the *Sun* the most successful newspaper of its time, and Day extraordinarily rich.

In the two hundred years since Day, technological innovation has altered how information is delivered. The mode of distribution evolved from newspapers to radio and TV, and to the Internet. What hasn't changed, however, is the unrelenting greed for human attention, and the methods used to mine it. Negativity, drama, sensationalism, and spectacle—essential ingredients of creating news with mass appeal—have remained unchanged.

There is a deep psychological principle at work here: Exposure to negativity makes people feel powerless. And when people feel that way, they engage in stress-relieving behaviors, such as compulsive buying and consuming.

Facebook, and now, many other social media platforms, have taken attention mining to a new level with their clever deployment of technology. They exploit both the basic human need to connect with others and the human addiction to variable rewards. (You get a ding on your phone. What could it be? A comment, a like, an expression of admiration? Well, you won't know until you check!) The ability to tie users to their feeds for hours is what makes Facebook more valuable than Walmart.

If you are serious about spiritual growth, you need to reclaim and preserve your attention, which requires creating a healthy relationship with information by cultivating the conscious and careful consumption of it.

Here are steps for an information detox:

1. Stop using mass media for 30 days. This includes news, TV, and social media.

2. Restrict your recreational internet use to a maximum of 30 minutes a day. Use the internet for essential activities only, such as work.

3. After 30 days, assess what you have learned from the exercise. You will likely find that you have not missed much. You may have enjoyed more time engaged in meaningful activities, and you likely feel more focused and relaxed.

4. Once the detox is over, you can let mass media channels re-enter your life. However, make sure they serve genuine needs. For each mass media source you want to reintroduce, write down what needs it serves and your rules of engagement (e.g., *I will watch a Netflix movie on Friday night, but only with friends*).

3. Emotion Detox

To be human is to know joy and sorrow, elation and heartbreak, passion and depression. There is nothing *inherently* wrong with negative emotions such as anger, fear, and sadness. They serve a crucial purpose: they are biologically hard-wired guidance mechanisms designed to move you away from harm and toward safety. As crude a mechanism as it may be, emotion is a gift to help us navigate the human journey.

The problem is when emotions linger long after the circumstances that produced them have gone away. Negative emotions, such as fear, secrete cortisol and other stress hormones into the bloodstream. These hormones prepare your body for the "fight or flight" response, which is exactly what you need when you are in real danger. However, if you are not truly in danger—and for those of us living in developed nations, we rarely are—prolonged exposure to stress hormones can cause immunodeficiency, high blood pressure, anxiety, insomnia, and heart problems. Therefore, getting rid of emotional toxicity is essential for your physical, emotional, and spiritual well-being.

There are three main sources of emotional toxicity—unresolved issues from trauma, unresolved grief, and persistent emotional conflicts. These unhealed wounds fester and create negative emotions.

Many people unconsciously repress their negative emotions. This is often caused by growing up in an environment where expressions of emotion were discouraged and became a defense mechanism. Repressing emotions does not get rid of them; instead, it pushes them below conscious awareness, where they fester in the psyche and create negative moods. When people don't express emotions, they try to mask the underlying discomfort through distractions, often in the form of drugs, work, or even an excessive drive to succeed.

Additionally, you might be in a toxic environment in which you face invalidation, negativity, criticism, or outright hostility. Toxic relationships characterized by manipulation, emotional abuse, constant criticism, or a lack of boundaries are examples. Staying in an environment where you feel unsupported or unappreciated can lead to overwhelming emotional distress.

The length of the journey to emotional well-being depends on how much emotional toxicity you have experienced. The journey does require effort, but it is effort well spent. By becoming emotionally healthy, you can unlock an empowered and joyful state of being.

Here are the seven steps to emotional detox:

1. **Acknowledge your emotions.** The first step to solving a problem is to acknowledge it. By being honest with yourself and bringing clarity to the challenges you face, you begin the process of healing. In your journal, write down which emotions you experience most frequently.

2. **Uncover and examine the root causes of your negative emotions.** Negative emotions often arise from abuse, neglect, and unmet needs. For each emotion you wrote in Step 1, add why you think you are feeling the negative emotion now (the proximate cause), then dig deeper to examine its root causes. This allows objective reflection

and brings the causes to awareness so they can be healed. For this step, it is important to avoid *rumination,* which is the tendency to play the mental tape of your past over and over. Rumination is counterproductive and drowns you further in negative emotions.

3. **Examine your beliefs.** Negative emotions are supported by limiting beliefs. For each emotion you listed before, write down the limiting beliefs that you suspect are causing the emotion. As an example, let's look at the power of beliefs in a story of heartbreak.

> Bob and Alice are a couple. Despite Bob's deep love for Alice, Alice decides to leave him. Bob is devastated. After he recovers from the initial shock, however, Bob realizes his depression is less about the loss of love than it is about the loss of his self-worth. When Alice left, Bob saw it as an unmistakable sign that he is flawed. This belief in his unworthiness prevents him from healing and moving on.
>
> If Bob works with his beliefs, he can adopt a healthier belief: that his worth is not dependent on approval from Alice, nor anyone else. After all, whether Alice left or stayed, Bob is still the same person. By acknowledging that his worth is independent of external approval, Bob is empowered to understand that Alice's choices were driven by her own motivations, and he can move on.

4. **Forgive.** The journey to healing begins with forgiveness. When we forgive, we release the source of our wounds. This process involves actively forgiving both yourself and others for transgressions. From a spiritual perspective, true forgiveness lies in the realization that *there is nothing to forgive.* Beneath the human form, you are an indestructible consciousness. By realizing your indestructibility, you can reframe pain into growth opportunities. To help you

forgive, you can do a special meditation that works at the level of samskaras. (This meditation, "Forgiveness and healing," is available for free on Children of Infinity's community page.) Unless those energetic patterns are cleansed and healed, the symptoms will keep appearing. Write down the names of people you need to forgive, then consciously forgive them.

5. **Get help.** If you find you are unable to heal psychological wounds using the steps above, seek professional help just as you would if you were physically injured. It is unfortunate that stigma prevents many people from seeking help for psychological problems. If you are serious about healing and moving on, get professional help immediately. Schedule time on your calendar to do research and make an appointment.

6. **Improve your physical health with exercise and rest.** The body and the mind are intimately connected: an unhealthy body creates negative moods. This is because it produces an insufficient quantity of neurotransmitters—the chemicals that create healthy emotions. The body produces these chemicals naturally when you exercise. Studies done with clinically depressed patients show that consistent exercise is as effective as antidepressant drugs for treatment, without any of the side effects. In addition to exercise, make sure that you get adequate rest. Fatigue makes the brain unhealthy and can lead to anxiety, addictions, and depression. Don't let your good intentions fall prey to the whims of your week: schedule exercise and rest on your calendar.

7. **Cultivate spiritual understanding.** The root cause of all suffering is spiritual ignorance. The external circumstances of your life, whether comfortable or not, are merely steppingstones to spiritual growth. You are a being of light—eternal and indestructible. True

spiritual understanding anchors you in peace that is unruffled by external conditions. You can develop a greater spiritual understanding through the discipline of daily study. For the next 30 days, read from a spiritually uplifting book and think about how this book can help you to create a better spiritual identity. An empowered spiritual identity will help you experience higher states of being, such as peace, joy, and contentment.

4. Relationship Detox

Your relationships affect you profoundly: those closest to you influence how you see reality, how you perceive your power, and how you make choices. This type of influence is evident, for instance, in a study published in 2007 in the *New England Journal of Medicine*. The study found that obesity spreads through close relationships. If one of your close friends becomes obese, there is a 57% chance you will too, which is a significant increase compared to the baseline. Your relationships exert a powerful pull on the quality and direction of your life.

The foundational insight for detoxing relationships is to understand the three levels of consciousness people manifest. These are:

1. **Tamas:** Tamasic people pull you into lower consciousness due to their negativity. Some of them are highly intelligent but use their intelligence to justify their powerlessness. They constantly complain and are full of resentment, jealousy, anger, and anguish. They relish gossip and tear others down. Most people find that this is the biggest bucket of the three.

2. **Rajas:** These people exude passion and energy, but the underlying driver is ego. As a result, you will find they are consumed with greed and a need for superiority. They often

exhibit agitation, overactivity, and the need to control.

3. **Sattva:** These people exude the quiet strength of peace. They present an example of how uplifting life can be; thus, they inspire you. A sign of people in this category is that they work on themselves and are more concerned with the internal world of mind, wisdom, and understanding. They constantly invest to make themselves better by reading, attending seminars and workshops, and being part of conscious communities. Many of them organize community initiatives to uplift others.

Here is the first step to detoxifying your relationships: Beginning with your closest relationships, then expanding to casual relationships, think of each person you know, and place them under one of the three types outlined above.

Here is the second step: Invest in relationships only with people in the Sattva category and respectfully distance yourself from people in the other two.

If you do not have many people who exhibit Sattva in your close circle, don't be discouraged. As the consciousness of our planet is rising, there are more and more people who are attracted to Sattva, and they are, by nature, nonjudgmental and accepting of others. There might already be communities of such people that you can find online or in person through local meditation centers or spiritual retreat centers. As you elevate your consciousness, you can also organize such communities and be a source of light to others.

Conclusion

In a world moving at dizzying speed, where we are incessantly bombarded by information, expectations, and the latest fads, it's easy to become burdened with what does not serve us. Over time, this accumulation of mental, physical, and emotional toxins leaves us stuck, exhausted, and unable to devote resources to what really matters: inner growth. To live your highest life, it is crucial to intentionally let go of what hinders your growth.

Detoxifying yourself from these burdening influences even once is a big step, but it's not something you can do once and never again. I recommend that you detox all aspects of your life at least once a year. By creating a conscious process, you will be able to design a life aligned with meaning and joy.

DeBORAH'S JOURNEY

Spiritual transformation leads to belonging—without which you might feel like a misfit. DeBorah speaks about the separation of her human and spiritual self before being united through authentic spirituality.

My entire life had been an attempt to fit in, spiritually and otherwise. I failed miserably at it. When I was six years old, I prepared to be baptized into the Church of Christ, which claimed to be the one true church possessing a ticket to heaven. While others may have felt privileged to be inducted into the ranks, even at this young age I questioned why this priceless gift was only given to such a select group in Houston, Texas. What about my friends in school or people living in Dallas or California? Surely "the chosen" would include more people than just those in our quaint congregation. But instead of getting answers, I got into serious trouble.

My connection with spirit manifested early in my life. As a child, I had prophetic dreams. At first, my family ignored them as fantasies. Then, they ordered me not to speak about my dreams for three days, and later, seven days, so I would forget them. Then I had a dream about my mother's death, which I described in detail, including the color of the walls in the room in which she would die, which were different from the walls in our house. Two weeks later, when the dream came true, my family told me I had attracted the tragedy. So, I learned to keep my mouth shut and ignore my spiritual gifts.

I have spent a lifetime with an unsettled spirit, unsatisfied with well-meaning but ineffective religious doctrines. I have been a Christian Scientist, a Catholic, and a Baptist before becoming non-denominational in my thirties. I searched for answers to questions I no longer dared speak aloud, such as: *Why would God only allow deacons and priests to understand and interpret His Word—what about the rest of us?* And, having felt the Holy Spirit energetically, *how does it work?*

My outer life, too, has been that of a misfit. Getting an education was a struggle. I was born to a teenage mother, so my rearing fell primarily on my grandmother's shoulders. This separation from my mother, followed by the death of my grandfather, would become a recurring theme of unreconciled loss in my life. My mother had two more babies before dying in childbirth only two weeks after the tragic passing of her husband. I carried the financial burden of helping my younger siblings as my grandmother's health declined, but my inquisitive spirit refused to surrender—I received my bachelor's while working full time and supporting my family.

When I began working with young men battling cancer on the floor of the MD Anderson Cancer Center, my relationship with death had already become complicated. As I watched families sell their homes to afford treatment for a disease that would often return, I frequently broke down with them at the hospital. Realizing that my compassionate nature was a liability there, I left my job in healthcare to pursue a master's degree in health education, with aspirations of becoming a school principal. This remained an unfulfilled goal, however, as poor management and corruption within the school system made me wary of accepting a school posting.

As I tried out various religions and jobs, yet remained a misfit, my spirit eventually began leaving my body. At first this happened with out-of-body experiences at night, which would leave me exhausted during the day. I was restless, as my spirit would leave me and be reluctant to rejoin my body once morning came. As my life became even more traumatic, the experiences started happening during daytime. Once, it happened while I was driving. I think this was an exit point to get out of this reality, but my love for my children prevented it, and I drove to safety. When the experience happened again, I stopped driving altogether.

It was clear my human life had become too traumatic for my spiritual self. I felt that my spirit and my earthly reality were experiencing a deep disconnect, which was in desperate need of repair. I began to search voraciously for answers regarding spirituality. The breakthrough happened in 2020 when I found Children of Infinity. I started meditating, reading, and learning about energy, which strengthened my spirit and understanding. I no longer needed to live in fear of what I did not understand, nor stay confused about my reality. With help from the energetic meditations offered by Dr. Narayan, I learned how to protect my energy field and provide nourishment to my spirit. Within a few months, I began driving again and found it such a treat!

Your soul isn't meant to languish in starvation and turmoil. Although hard to find, authentic spiritual tools exist even today. By using them, you can create a healthy and positive environment in which you can flourish.

May your spirit thrive!

DeBorah Flowers is the Children of Infinity community leader for the Midwest region. She lives in Houston, Texas.

Step 4: Channel Higher Energies

"The intuitive mind is a sacred gift and the rational mind is a faithful servant. We have created a society that honors the servant and has forgotten the gift."

—Albert Einstein

"You are not IN the universe, you ARE the universe, an intrinsic part of it. Ultimately, you are not a person, but a focal point where the universe is becoming conscious of itself. What an amazing miracle."

—Eckhart Tolle

A helpful way to understand your spiritual ability is to view yourself as a *transformer of Source Energy*.

An electrical transformer takes in electricity and changes its voltage. The transformer can raise voltage (think of huge industrial transformers that power heavy machinery), or it can reduce it (think of small ones that charge cell phones). In a similar fashion, you transform universal energy and channel it to *create* through you. What you create is informed by the level of your consciousness.

This chapter provides the conceptual tools necessary for understanding how to use universal energy to manifest your highest life.

Your Partnership with the Universe

In Step 1, we delved into how Unity fragments into Infinity, with each portion of consciousness contributing to the shared mission: evolution through incarnations.

To make the most of your journey, it's essential to grasp some key spiritual concepts—the Higher Self, pre-birth planning, the Veil, and the flow of inspiration. Understanding how they work together can help you tap into the universe's guidance and support. I will discuss these, and important related concepts, below.

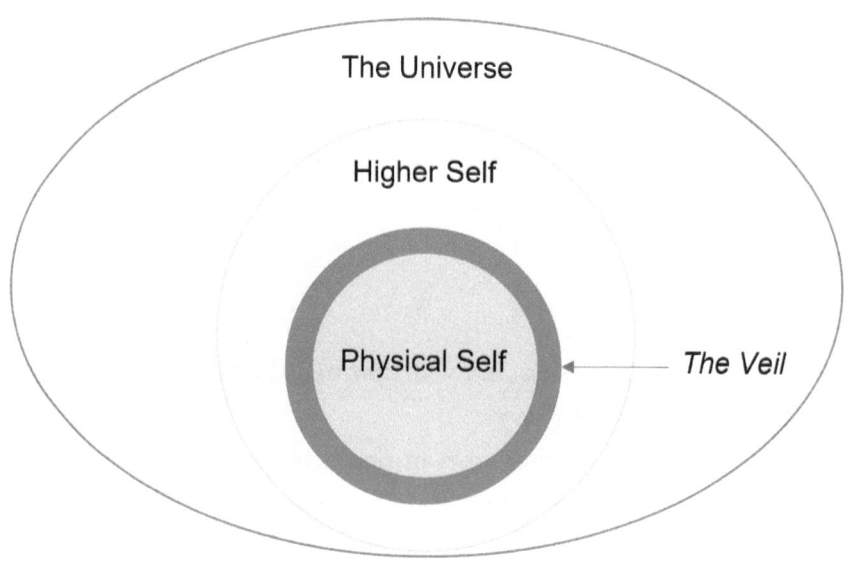

The Universe

Think of the universe as a conscious being with an infinitely large body (body of Source, if you will). Out of this boundless awareness arises the individual, non-physical consciousness known as your Higher Self. Your Higher Self, in turn, guides and shapes your physical, incarnated self—the "you" experiencing life here and now.

In this sacred collaboration, the universe operates as a masterful architect, weaving together the perfect circumstances for your growth through synchronicity. Like pieces of a puzzle falling into place, the right people, opportunities, and events arrive at precisely the right moment.

Yet, this cosmic intelligence works subtly, always honoring your free will. Its imperceptible hand moves behind the scenes, ensuring that its guidance never feels like coercion. This is why we often mistake synchronicity for coincidence—its gentle touch is designed not to overwhelm or control, but to support.

The Higher Self

The Higher Self is the non-physical part of you that is connected to the universe and all creation. It is the source of your intuition, your inner wisdom, and your spiritual guidance. This is your essence; it is aware of all your incarnations (which likely number in the hundreds), and it grows through all of them.

With a panoramic view of your soul's journey, your Higher Self understands your life's greater purpose, your innate gifts, and the lessons you're here to master. When you align with it, you tap into profound clarity and direction. A deep sense of trust arises—an inner knowing that everything is unfolding as it should. In this connection, you experience peace, fulfillment, and a quiet certainty that you are exactly where you need to be.

The Physical Self

Your physical self, the *body-mind,* is the most tangible part of the partnership. You perceive the world through your senses and make decisions based on your beliefs and awareness. The physical self navigates life using free will, which is an extremely powerful force that shapes reality with every decision, no matter how small. Even seemingly insignificant decisions, such as where you park your car, alter reality by limiting the choices of those who come to park after you. Each action sets in motion a cascade of cause and effect, weaving the tapestry of shared reality.

The physical self operates within constraints—bound by time, space, and the laws of cause and effect. It is also shaped by conditioning: habits, societal norms, and past experiences that shape your perception. In the rush of daily life, it's easy to lose touch with your Higher Self, becoming absorbed in the immediate struggles of the body-mind. But remember—you are never truly separate. Even in the densest moments of earthly experience, your eternal essence remains available, quietly guiding you back to alignment.

Pre-birth Planning

The co-creation between your physical self, Higher Self, and the universe begins long before birth. Decades of research into near-death experiences and past-life memories suggest that we consciously design our lives before incarnation. This may seem difficult to accept, especially when a lifetime includes hardships such as trauma or loss. Yet every experience, no matter how painful, serves as a catalyst for soul growth.

Before embodiment, your Higher Self sets the growth intention, a guiding purpose for this incarnation. The plan is designed within the framework of *probabilities,* not certainties, shaped by free will and the ever-shifting possibilities of physical existence. For example, you might choose Walter and Kim as potential parents, and they, in their own pre-birth planning, may agree to this arrangement. But once incarnated, their choices (and countless external factors) determine whether they actually meet, partner, or conceive. Your birth to them remains one potential path among many.

This inherent indeterminacy is fundamental to our universe. Nothing is rigidly predetermined—not just in our life plans, but in the very fabric of reality. Quantum physics reveals this at the subatomic level: particles exist in states of potential until observed or interacted with. Similarly, your incarnation unfolds through a dynamic interplay between soul intentions and free will.

A pre-birth plan is crafted to maximize soul's evolution during an incarnation. The plan includes the following details:

- Physical characteristics. Culture, birth conditions, race, and body type.

- Psychological aspects and the belief systems you will be born into.

- Relationships, including parents, partners, and children. (Yes, *you chose your parents for this lifetime.* Although you may not have a positive relationship with them, they agreed to serve as your parents and provide the experiences you need on your journey.)

- Life themes. These are the lessons you want to learn (forgiveness, leadership, balance, and so on) and how you will learn them (work with people, machines or ideas, and so on). Depending on the lessons, you also choose opportunities (e.g., to be born within a well-to-do family) and challenges (e.g., having a physical disability).

- Gifts, such as healing, intuition, or artistic ability. As you grow through incarnations, you master a variety of skills. During an incarnation, you might work with only some of these gifts to focus on a specific lesson.
- Purpose and mission for a lifetime.

It's crucial to understand that pre-birth planning is not fatalism or predestination. Rather, it's a flexible, co-creative process where your soul sets key intentions and learning objectives while leaving room for infinite possibilities based on free will. Think of it like planning a road trip—you might choose your destination and pack certain supplies, but the route you take, the detours you encounter, and the people you meet along the way remain fluid based on your choices.

Here are three books you can read to learn more about pre-birth planning:

1. *Memories of the Afterlife* from the Newton Institute
2. *Messages from the Masters* by Dr. Brian Weiss
3. *Your Soul's Gift* by Robert Schwartz

The Veil

During incarnation, a mechanism called *the Veil* partially blocks your awareness of your Higher Self and your true nature. But why would your soul willingly choose such forgetfulness? Because true growth requires authentic engagement—the kind that only happens when the stakes feel real.

Compare the experience of flying an airplane with operating a perfect flight simulator. Though your senses can't tell the difference between the two, knowing the simulator isn't real changes everything. You would not have the same focus if you were aware of the "safety net."

While it restricts direct access to your Higher Self, the Veil is permeable. As you evolve spiritually, the Veil becomes thinner, which enables you to tap into clear guidance and support from your Higher Self. You become more intuitive, and your life acquires a quality of ease. This doesn't mean you won't face challenges; rather, you will navigate through them with poise and inner assurance.

The Veil, then, is love in action—a divine gift that makes your earthly journey not just a test, but a revelation in progress.

The False Self, or Ego

During an incarnation, the physical self, temporarily veiled from of its connection to Source Energy, adopts the identity of the false self, also referred to as the ego (distinct from the Freudian concept of ego). The false self is created by mistaking yourself for the body-mind and its constructs, such as beliefs, fears, desires, and your familial and social roles. Unlike the expansive, fluid nature of your true self, the false self resists change and seeks control.

The false self is not innate, it is created from conditioning. The two strongest forms of conditioning are:

1. **Biological conditioning.** As previously discussed in the evolution of densities, the human self evolves from the second-density *animal self,* which is fundamentally driven by the need for survival, safety, and security. While these instincts are essential for physical existence, over-identification with them keeps consciousness trapped in basic needs, making it difficult to pursue higher spiritual growth and contribute to a conscious, compassionate society.

2. **Social conditioning.** From birth, our thoughts, values, and behaviors are shaped by external influences—parents, education

systems, religious doctrines, and cultural narratives. For example, modern Western society conditions people to equate success with material wealth, consumerism, and social status, often at the expense of inner fulfillment and authentic purpose. As a result, many pursue careers, relationships, and lifestyles that align with external validation rather than soul-aligned truth.

When dominated by the false self, the incarnated being becomes ensnared in misguided pursuits, mistaking power, control, or material accumulation for true fulfillment. The tragedy of the false self is that it obscures the truth: You are not the ego—you are the awareness that observes it.

The path to liberation isn't about destroying the false self but seeing through it. By questioning our conditioning, we can peel back the layers of illusion and remember our eternal nature as expressions of Source.

Personality

In addition to ego, the physical self creates a personality with unique characteristics that determine how you perceive and interact with life. Extroverted and introverted characteristics, for example, have unique strengths and advantages. People with extroverted personalities can move easily in social situations. They enjoy a variety of social groups and love communicating verbally, and they are likely comfortable taking risks. People with introverted personalities often have a strong ability to focus and pay attention to detail. They tend to be independent thinkers and have fewer but deeper relationships, and they are comfortable with solitude.

The key is to honor your authentic personality—not as a limitation, but as your soul's chosen way to uniquely navigate your journey.

Guidance from the Higher Self

If free will allows us to wander off course, how does an incarnation stay aligned with our soul's purpose?

Here is how: through inner guidance, which is ever-present. In order to respect free will, however, this guidance must be gentle. We often want a higher power to tell us what to do in every difficult situation, but such guidance would overpower our free will.

The gentle way in which guidance shows up is through inspiration. You might be taking a walk when an idea comes to start a business, learn something new, or share your gifts. Since the guidance mechanism is subtle, it is easy to ignore these ideas or tell yourself they are impractical. If you act on them, however, you will find the universe opens doors for you through synchronicity—events, people, and resources show up in your life at the right time so you can progress toward your heartfelt goals. People often use the word *coincidence*, but once you mature spiritually, you understand there are no coincidences, only orchestration from the universe.

Whether to seize a given inspiration is a decision guided by your free will. Openness and trust are required to receive guidance and move forward.

In lower states of consciousness, when life is ruled by fear, you are likely to ignore inspiration and cling to the status quo. If gentle guidance goes unheeded, the universe can intervene more directly, giving you a gentle push. Your Higher Self agreed upon these course corrections (which often appear as crises) as part of your pre-birth plan. Your relationship may suddenly fall apart, or you may face a health issue that forces you to reexamine your life, or your job may cease to exist. The crisis may seem a devastating blow, but you later realize it wasn't a blow at all, only the push you needed to achieve your life's purpose.

As you awaken, you learn to collaborate with the universe. You begin to trust that the universe conspires in your favor and that every experience is a lesson to help you grow and evolve. You release your rigid expectations and surrender to the flow of life.

Listening to and working with your inspiration is a crucial skill on the spiritual journey. It is to create a better connection to your Higher Self that we meditate and go within. By acting on your inspiration, you align with higher purpose and radiate light to inspire others.

A Story of Acting on Inspiration

Life does not happen to *you; it happens* for *you. It is a sacred dance that leads to greater joy, wisdom, and higher consciousness.*

Acting on your inspiration can open doors to invaluable gifts and your highest life. Let me tell you a story relevant to this insight—about how Children of Infinity came to be.

In November 2019, I found myself browsing Facebook, a site I had not used for years. I came across the profile of Obaidur, an acquaintance from college I hadn't been in touch with since 2003. I learned he had moved to Germany and started a yoga community, offering yoga classes in a park without sign-ups or fees.

Obaidur's story stirred something deep within me. I asked myself —what if I could similarly share what I had learned on my spiritual quest of two decades?

At first, the thought was no more than a fantasy. I had to consider the facts that made me clearly unsuitable for being a spiritual teacher: I was (and still am) an introvert. I had a heavy Indian accent, no knowledge of webinar technology, and a mortal fear of the camera. I also was not sure about what to share. I lived in the United States, a foreign country rooted in a different spiritual belief system, and although interest in non-duality was growing, it was mostly confined to academic spheres in science and philosophy. It was clear that my teachings would face resistance.

The bigger issue was that my responsibilities—caring for young children, leading a software team, managing an investment property, and maintaining my personal spiritual practice—left me with no time. Yet, here came the unsolicited call of inspiration. It would have been easy to tell myself that I did not have the skills to present ideas about spirituality, but the inspiration nonetheless took root.

I explored a bit and found a webinar platform to share a basic presentation with text and my voice. I then created a local group on Meetup.com to share. When a few dozen people showed up to listen, they did not care about my accent, that I was unknown, or that I had unconventional ideas about spirituality. They thanked me for overcoming my fears and said they wanted to learn more. The humble beginning opened doors to what happened in the next few years:

1. Within two months, the COVID pandemic hit, and the world was locked down. When the ceaseless outer activity stopped, people had time to go within. Further, as virtual meetings became the norm, I could reach a worldwide audience. I learned how to create videos with simple animations and share my message using YouTube Telecast for free.

2. The lockdown afforded me time to refine my ideas and create a body of work that would serve as a foundation for my teachings. As the community grew, I created Children of Infinity, a non-profit dedicated to serving lightworkers.

3. My investments did well enough to create a financial cushion. That enabled me to take a salary cut, reduce working hours, and devote more time to helping the non-profit.

4. I was inspired to move to California because of the milder weather and greater concentration of spiritual communities. My

wife and I traveled there and put in an offer on a house. It was an insane seller's market, and the home got seventeen other offers in a single day, but the owners decided to accept our offer.

5. The greatest gift I received was guidance from people with extraordinary abilities. I encountered John Chandler and learned how to channel energy from the non-physical realm. His guidance enabled me to become a conduit for energies from Goddess Saraswati, the individuated portion of Source that represents Universal Intelligence. In ancient Eastern texts, she is referred to as the Goddess of Wisdom. After a few months, I began channeling energies from other beings, including Lakshmi, Durga, and Divine Mother.

My story is a testament to the power of following your inspiration. I am in no way unique; every human is endowed with transformative spiritual abilities. To claim them, however, we must demonstrate courage by taking action. In its infinite wisdom, the universe doesn't force gifts upon us. Instead, it waits patiently, trusting that one day we will mature and claim our birthright.

Inspiration vs. Ego Chatter

A crucial skill on the path is the ability to differentiate inspiration from the voice of ego.

The term *ego chatter* refers to ego's fearful, needy, restless, and greedy voice. The chatter creates the *monkey mind*—the mind jumps from thought to thought just like a monkey jumping from branch to branch. Since ego chatter and inspiration both come from the mind, how can you differentiate them?

This discernment may be challenging, especially if you have not trained your mind to examine energetic patterns of thoughts. But it is a skill that can be developed with practice. Here are some insights to begin:

- Ego is driven by the need for safety, survival, and security; inspiration is driven by the higher needs of meaning, purpose, and contribution.

- Ego seeks validation by accumulating external symbols of power, such as money, influence, and fame; inspiration expresses the authentic self, which provides validation from within. For example, if you feel the desire to paint, your ego may do so to seek recognition, an external reward. Inspiration, on the other hand, seeks to express your creativity without needing any external validation: *you paint because it brings you joy.*

- Ego is driven by the need to conform and seeks what is popular; inspiration seeks to express your authentic individuality.

- Ego generates negative emotions such as fear, doubt, and judgment; inspiration uplifts and offers a vision of who you could be—not as seen through the social mirror (what others think of you), but how you see yourself.

Trusting Your Partnership with Your Higher Self

Your ability to act on inspiration is determined by your level of trust. As a human being, your biological need for security and stability creates an invisible prison—a comfort zone—around you. You do not grow when you stay within it, so your Higher Self attempts to get you out of it.

Living an inspired life requires taking risks and trying things that may not work. But that's better than staying within your comfort zone, where no growth happens. Being stuck in the familiar patterns of your routine creates boredom, complacency, and a lack of fulfillment.

When you step outside your comfort zone, you open yourself up to new experiences, challenges, and opportunities. This can be scary and uncomfortable at first, but it offers priceless opportunities for learning, development, and personal transformation. As you venture further, you sharpen your skills, gain confidence, and expand your vision. Your passion helps you connect with like-minded individuals. By taking risks and trying new things, you can design a life aligned with your authentic self and reach your highest potential.

How to Develop Trust

So, how do you develop trust in yourself and the universe?

The first step is to acquire spiritual knowledge. Trust begins with *knowing*—understanding the deeper architecture of your existence. By studying concepts, such as reincarnation and pre-birth planning, you realize that life is not a random accident but a sacred collaboration with the universe. The universe is actively supporting you, so there is nothing to be afraid of.

Second, act on whatever inspiration you already have to the best of your ability. The universe, acting as a wise teacher, gives you small bits of inspiration before giving you bigger ones. Trust is like a muscle: it becomes stronger with use. Often, the problem is not a lack of inspiration but a lack of action. When you act on the nudges you have received, no matter how small, the universe opens more doors—with synchronicities and deeper guidance. Over time, the inspirations grow clearer, and your path unfolds with effortless flow.

The secret is to start where you are. Be willing to make mistakes and look foolish when you answer the call of inner guidance. You can nurture your spirit by not taking opinions, even your own, too seriously. Value perspectives, but don't be constrained by them.

In the larger scheme of things, you will notice that there are no mistakes. What seems to be a mistake today could be the intermediate step you need to achieve your goal. In the chapters that follow, I will outline a detailed plan of daily activities that will help you live an inspired life.

EXERCISE
Understand Your Partnership with the Universe

1. Recall the most positive shifts in your life. These might include meeting a soul-aligned partner, finding purposeful work, or discovering a passion that lights you up. What subtle nudges or intuitions preceded these changes?

2. Think of the things you're happiest about in your life right now. For each one, make a list of all the things that had to *go right* to get you to where you are today. Do you see how the invisible hand of the universe has played a part in bringing them about?

3. To view your journey from a higher perspective, reflect on your most challenging experiences in this lifetime. How have those experiences helped you grow and contributed to a deeper life?

ADELA'S JOURNEY

Spiritual transformation can bridge the gap between seemingly contradictory ideas. Adela shares how bridging the gap between science and spirituality, along with upgrading her leadership model, has enabled her to pursue her purpose.

From a very young age, my life has been one of contradiction between my authentic self and the cultural microcosm. My early life in a small Argentinian town was a portrait of the Catholic way of life juxtaposed against my innate talents of clairvoyance and my intellectual attraction to science. After all, as anyone who's ever heard the joke knows—when a scientist, a Catholic, and a clairvoyant walk into a bar, you can rest assured they did not come there together. Unable to reconcile my gifts with my cultural and familial norms, and lacking any opportunity to develop them, I respectfully requested that my spiritual gifts be taken from me. My spirit guides agreed, and I became "normal."

I spent the next few decades pursuing higher education, eventually earning a PhD in computer science before settling in the United States and securing a job at Arizona State University. I was happily married and achieved success in academia. However, as I progressed in my career and was offered leadership opportunities, I turned them down because, once again, I struggled with contradicting beliefs. Leadership, I thought, consists of task-driven aggression and authority, which I value little. Unable to reconcile the contradiction, I declined this gift of leadership.

My life changed dramatically after the sudden passing of my husband during COVID. Longing to feel his presence, I submitted to my spirit guides that my childhood gifts be returned. With my abilities restored and the gate to intuition reopened, I was again immersed in a world of contradiction between my empirical training as a scientist and my innate abilities as an intuitive. This time, however, I was guided so I could reconcile the contradiction. As synchronicity unfolded in my life, a colleague told me about Children of Infinity and Dr. K Narayan's scientific approach to spirituality. I eagerly accepted the opportunity to learn and be guided.

I discovered that my conflicting ideas of science and spirituality arose because the only model of spirituality I knew had been based on religion. I liked that Dr. Narayan used his background in physics to present a non-dogmatic view of spirituality and encouraged us to research and form our own opinions. The books he recommended were written by PhDs and MDs, people I could relate to. It was in this reconciliation that my transformation began, and along with it, my soul purpose was revealed. I was to be the voice of the voiceless, and what's more, I was to lead others in this undertaking. Still, I faced the issue of aggressive leadership, and I was still uneasy with leadership in general.

During a yearlong study group with Children of Infinity, I was tasked by my peers to describe how I perceived the pillars of leadership. My answer included words such as *dominance, intolerance,* and *control.* It became clear why I had such an issue accepting leadership positions. I was then tasked with describing the beliefs and values I would bring to a leadership position. I answered with words like *compassion, care,* and *support.* The exercise helped me realize that leadership could be based on kindness rather than aggression.

In 2023, I enrolled in a course on spiritual leadership by Dr. Narayan. I learned that authentic leadership is founded upon compassion and a desire to serve, as displayed by great leaders such as Lincoln and Gandhi. Once again, I realized that a limiting belief system was holding me back from my leadership journey.

As another play of synchronicity, no sooner had the course concluded than I was offered an opportunity to lead a nationwide effort to help underrepresented people. This time, I accepted.

I now preside over a national leadership cohort at my university, where I co-lead the extension of the National Institute of Drug Abuse Clinical Trial Network at Arizona State University. My leadership in this endeavor is decidedly driven by compassionate energy. I aim to continue leading with compassion and dedicating myself to a leadership model aligned with feminine qualities.

In retrospect, it was only after aligning my spiritual beliefs with scientific principles that I could tap into greater parts of my being. That connection enabled me to receive the guidance I needed. I followed Dr. Narayan's recommended practices to raise my vibration. I stopped eating meat, which was no small feat coming from a Latin background, and I have drastically reduced my consumption of social media and news. Instead of engaging in these vibration-lowering activities, I meditate, exercise, and read daily. As a result, the channel of guidance has opened for me in a way that I am given answers rather than contradictions. I've made a habit of writing questions in my journal before going to sleep and eagerly awaiting the answers, which often come during sleep or meditation.

I find great joy in what the universe chooses to send me now that I reside in a state of peace. I will continue my efforts to reduce suffering as I serve a higher purpose.

Adela Grando is an award-winning professor and Director of Research Education at the College of Health Solutions, Arizona State University.

Step 5: Cultivate Daily Spiritual Practice

"Practice is the hardest part of learning, and training is the essence of transformation."

—Ann Voskamp

"An ounce of practice is generally worth more than a ton of theory."

—E. F. Schumacher

We all carry infinite spiritual potential within, but it takes showing up—day after day, week after week—to transform that potential into reality. Consistent, intentional effort is the bridge that takes us from where we are to where we want to be.

Practice is powerful because it rewires the brain. When we practice something consistently, whether it's meditating or playing the piano, we strengthen specific neural pathways. Over time, these pathways become more efficient, making the activity feel easier and more natural. Someone new to meditation may find it hard to sit still for five minutes, but with regular practice, the brain adapts, and what once required conscious effort becomes second nature. Seasoned meditators can enter a state of effortless, focused calm and stay there for hours.

One of the great discoveries in the human potential movement is that mastery is the result of deliberate practice. Malcolm Gladwell popularized the idea of the "10,000-hour rule," suggesting that it takes roughly 10,000 hours of practice to achieve mastery in any field. While the exact number is debated, the underlying principle holds true: mastery requires time, effort, and persistence.

On the spiritual path, the goal is to elevate our consciousness and improve the mind, which acts as a lens through which we see the world. By focusing on training the mind, instead of pursuing external things we think will make us happy, we transform the way we experience life.

Over time, these practices lead to a profound shift in consciousness. We become less reactive and more responsive, less attached to external outcomes and more grounded in inner peace. Spiritual practice helps us transcend the ego and access higher states of awareness, in which we experience unity, compassion, and unconditional love. Our relationship with our fellow human beings transforms because the tendency to judge others diminishes. We also develop the inner strength to go through the inevitable trials of the human journey.

I will focus on three core spiritual practices in this chapter: spiritual study, meditation, and self-inquiry.

Spiritual Study

Spiritual study is the disciplined process of learning about spiritual principles, the nature of existence, and how to live an enlightened life.

We explored the power of beliefs in Step 1. Your spiritual worldview, as I emphasized, is largely a product of your culture. The simplest way to change your worldview is by studying books and other materials that offer you an alternate, higher spiritual perspective. For example, by learning about other people's near-death experiences, your own fear of death can diminish. Similarly, learning about pre-birth planning enables you to stop seeing your challenges as random phenomena happening to you and, instead, see them as gifts meant to assist your growth. As you continue the practice of spiritual study, your disempowering beliefs will gradually be replaced with empowering ones, creating the foundation for enlightened living.

The most important principle of spiritual study is that *study should lead to transformation, not merely knowledge.* In the age of information overload, it is easy to become a consumer of spiritual information rather than a student of spiritual wisdom. Media platforms, such as YouTube, offer thousands of hours of *free* content that anyone with an internet connection can watch. But it's a trap designed to turn you into an information addict. Mindlessly consuming information does not lead to enlightenment, only to confusion and the loss of your most important resource: time.

To use study as a transformative spiritual tool, commit to depth. Instead of studying a lot of material, narrow your effort to study only a few high-quality books a year. Don't read them as you read a novel, but do the difficult work needed to integrate the learning and make it a part of your life.

The best way to deepen learning is by using a journal. Use it to write what you have learned, create specific action steps to implement, and keep track of such actions.

EXERCISE
Read Spiritual Books

1. Explore Children of Infinity's handpicked list of books at https://childrenofinfinity.org/recommendations/.
You can also join study groups in our online community at https://childrenofinfinity.org

2. Choose a book to study.

3. Create a daily routine to read for 15-30 minutes.

Meditation

"Most people believe the mind to be a mirror, more or less accurately reflecting the world outside them, not realizing on the contrary that the mind is itself the principal element of creation."

—Rabindranath Tagore

All human experience—the heavenly ecstasy, the unbearable agony, and everything in between—comes from the mind.

The mind doesn't merely perceive reality; no, it creates reality. Reality is not what you see with your eyes and touch with your fingers, but the story the mind tells about what is seen and touched. And therein lies the key to true freedom.

To stop being a victim of the mind's creations, we first must *become mindful of the mind,* which is precisely what meditation helps us achieve.

Meditation helps us become aware of the inner workings of the mind, which operates like a computer. Similar to software, mental programs create mental and emotional outcomes. The trouble is that the computer has a mind of its own: it runs unpleasant programs without our permission.

Worry is one such familiar program. Let's say you start worrying about the pain in your knee. Pretty soon, you wonder whether you need knee replacement surgery. You then start fretting about the out-of-control hospital bills, and that the catastrophic cost of surgery will put retirement out of reach. "Gosh, I work so hard!" you tell yourself, "Why doesn't the government fix the healthcare in this country?" The worry program has now spawned indignation. You are living in an emotional hell created by a runaway program in your mind.

If you are aware, however, you could notice when the program is about to run rampant. Awareness offers you a chance to stop before your mind enacts the full-blown melodrama.

During the past few decades, the practice of meditation has become popular because of brain research. Using advanced brain imaging technology, researchers have proven that meditation increases the amount of gray matter in the brain and helps with physiological functions, such as stress reduction and enhanced immunity. I can vouch from my own experience that prolonged spiritual practice creates a state of peace and harmony experienced within oneself and one's surroundings. This state of peace is not an emotion or a feeling (which both arise from physical stimuli) but an inner state that remains stable even in the midst of a busy life.

The Two Technologies of Meditation

Given the numerous types of meditation practiced around the world, what is the most effective kind?

To answer the question, we must understand what underlying technology is being used in a given meditation system. Despite the wide variety of techniques, there are only two broad approaches to meditation.

The first and most common kind—contemplative meditation—uses *the mind to transcend the mind.* The training is achieved by focusing the mind on an object or a process, such as an image, a mantra, or the breath. When focus is lost due to the mind's ceaseless wandering, the practice is to bring the attention back and continue to meditate. In the long term, the meditator reaps dual benefits—the mind wanders less, and attachment to thoughts diminishes. Contemplative meditation is the tool I used when I began my spiritual journey, and I continued in this way for fifteen long years before I even learned about an altogether different technology of meditation.

The second type, *energetic meditation,* uses energy to transform the mind. Since all of existence is energy, patterns such as thoughts, habits, and ways of interacting with reality are also energetic in nature. According to yoga philosophy, the energetic patterns that drive our behavior are called *samskaras* (seed patterns). Through energetic meditation, energy is used to change the samskaras, thus transforming the core of our being.

The reason energetic meditation is not common is that to receive such energy, you need a channel who can act as a conduit. It is for this reason that energetic meditation cannot be taught; *it must be transmitted.*

If you have not experienced energetic meditation before, this may sound like a strange fantasy, much as the idea of flying was two hundred years ago. You need to experience it to believe it. I have used both meditation technologies in my spiritual journey, and I have found energetic meditation to be revolutionary, much like switching from a bicycle to a car as a means of travel.

In my case, I was extremely fortunate to come across my teacher, John, who transmits energy from Divine Mother, the feminine aspect of Source. Through John's guidance, I have learned how to use Divine Mother's energy to create tools for spiritual growth and healing. If you have not worked with Divine Mother's energy before, I recommend using an energetic meditation called "Stairway of Light." During the

15-minute meditation, my voice acts as a channel for Divine Mother's energy, which infuses your chakras (energy centers) and unblocks your spiritual evolution. You can get the meditation from my audiobook, *Heal, Transform, Ascend: Breakthrough Energy Healing from Divine Mother.*

To benefit from Divine Mother's energy, you do not need special skills or training, just openness to the experience and a willingness to meditate daily. During the meditation, you may experience energy moving through your body, and you may see colors or hear sounds. It's a simple but powerful way to incorporate meditation into your daily routine.

Sacred Space

At its core, spiritual practice is energetic work. Over time, energy becomes anchored in physical space. That is why it is recommended to create a space exclusively for spiritual practice. A dedicated room is best, but if that is not possible, you can use a portion of a room, such as a corner. Keep it clean and orderly, and use objects you consider sacred to enhance your space. These might include symbols of enlightened beings, such as Divine Mother, Buddha, Jesus, or Krishna.

Time

Choose a set time to practice each day, when you will not be interrupted. According to yoga philosophy, the best time to meditate is between 3 a.m. and 6 a.m. This time period, known as *Brahma Muhurta*, is powerful because your connection to non-physical realms is strongest during the transition from sleep to waking up. But if the time is too early for you, don't worry. You can meditate immediately after waking up or just before going to bed, as the connection to the higher realms is still strong during these times.

Posture

Use a comfortable posture that enables you to stay still and fully present during your practice. Do not use advanced but uncomfortable yogic postures, as discomfort will prevent you from going within. The only requirement is that your spine must be kept straight because it acts as an energy conduit.

There are three recommended postures for meditation:

1. **Sit in a cross-legged position.** This is the ideal posture because it maximizes your contact with the earth, which acts as a reservoir of energy.

2. **Sit on a chair.** Use a chair that offers back support and ensure that your feet are flat on the ground.

3. **Lie down.** The corpse pose *(Shava Asana)* is perfect for meditating before going to sleep.

EXERCISE
Meditate

1. Get the guided meditation "Stairway of Light." Do this meditation every day upon waking up. As the morning practice becomes ingrained, gradually add a bedtime meditation practice.

2. Set a schedule to meditate every day at the same time.

Self-Inquiry

To live an enlightened life, we must make choices that honor ourselves and others. The reason we fail to do so is that we are prevented by unexamined patterns that operate below the level of conscious awareness. These patterns originate from biological and social programming. For example, you might have unconsciously learned avoidance because that's what you observed in your parents. Unless you become conscious of them, such patterns negatively affect your own relationships.

Self-inquiry forces the mind to examine its inner workings and illuminates unconscious patterns, enabling you to make decisions from higher states of consciousness. This may be difficult at first because our culture focuses on the external, and we are seldom taught to explore the inner world. Self-inquiry exposes uncomfortable inner patterns, also known as the *shadow self*. The shadow self consists of attributes that you consider undesirable, and so you hide them to avoid confronting them. For example, people who suffer from unworthiness engage in self-sabotage, so they don't have to confront why they feel unworthy.

Self-inquiry exposes your shadows, which may become emotionally and psychologically draining, leading you to abandon the work altogether. That's why it is critical to *observe yourself without judgment*. Such observation enables you to examine your choices and determine underlying causes without judgment or blame.

Self-Inquiry: An Example

Let's imagine that your partner accuses you of being a messy person. This accusation presents you with a choice between two paths. The first path reflects lower consciousness, rooted in fear and anger. Here are some common responses that arise from disempowering emotions and the abdication of responsibility:

- **Denial:** *What are you talking about? I didn't create a mess.*
- **Anger:** *How can you say that to me?*
- **Judgment:** *You always blame me instead of appreciating me.*
- **Counterattack:** *What about the mess you made that I had to clean up?*
- **Victimhood:** *You treat me so unfairly.*
- **Self-righteousness:** *I work so hard to make this partnership work. Why can't you give me a break?*

In contrast, a response aligned with higher consciousness is rooted in compassion, harmony, and peace. Someone responding from a state of higher consciousness might say, "Oh, honey, I'm sorry. I know you work so hard. I'll clean it up, and be more careful next time." This response immediately diffuses the situation, increases love between you and your partner, and allows your partner to reflect on their behavior. Aligning yourself with higher consciousness requires an impartial examination of your behavior, taking responsibility for it, and working to improve it.

Under the influence of ego, you tend to justify your mistakes. But by not doing so, you will have the creative space to solve problems and choose love and harmony.

The "How" of Self-Inquiry

Set aside ten minutes daily to sit in silence and reflect on the most important choices of the day. Do not categorize your choices as right or wrong because judgment adds unhelpful mental commentary and creates self-blame. Also, avoid playing the "poor me" tape when you observe that you made a poor choice. The tape may sound something like this:

- "How can I be so dumb?"
- "What can I do? I was so tired!"
- "I am a horrible person and don't deserve happiness."

Instead of playing the blame game, give yourself the gift of accurate, detached observations and probe your behaviors more deeply. For example, you might observe, *I chose to respond with anger. Let me examine why I did so without blaming myself or anyone else.*

As you dig deeper, you may notice patterns; for example, that you have difficulty responding to criticism. As you go even deeper, you may uncover a core belief. You might find you feel insecure, and, due to insecurity, you need others to acknowledge your worth. The discovery then spurs you to create a practice: when someone criticizes you, instead of reacting, you calm yourself and observe your behavior objectively. Are there things you should improve in your behavior?

Self-inquiry can be used for all kinds of choices, such as why you choose to stay with friends to have fun when you really want to go home and get rest or choose not to show up for a class that would have been valuable.

By consistently practicing self-inquiry, you can become more conscious of your choices and gradually learn to make better ones. The best way to do this is through journaling, which creates structured self-inquiry.

I suggest taking the following steps to create a daily journaling practice:

1. Choose a time of day to devote 5-10 minutes to writing without interruption.

2. Choose a specific area of your life that you want to explore in your journal, such as relationships, work, or personal growth.

3. Set an intention for your session, such as a question you want to explore or an insight you hope to gain.

4. Write without editing or censoring yourself. Allow your thoughts and feelings to flow freely onto the page.

5. Reflect on what you have written. Look for patterns, insights, and emerging themes, for example, a pattern of overcommitting.

6. Use what you have written as a basis for further inquiry. Ask yourself questions that delve deeper into the issues raised in your writing. For example, do you overcommit because you like to please others?

7. Use the insights you have gained from your journaling practice to create specific habits. Create a plan to implement changes based on what you have learned. Using the overcommitment example above, you may become more vigilant about checking your calendar and taking a moment to reflect before accepting an invitation.

With consistent journaling, you can identify behavioral patterns that do not align with higher consciousness and change them.

EXERCISE
Self-Inquiry

1. Set aside 5 minutes a day to practice self-inquiry.

2. Use a journal to assist your self-inquiry practice.

Support Your Spiritual Practice

A spiritually aligned lifestyle is paramount for accelerating your spiritual growth.

As discussed in Step 2, everything in the universe has an energetic signature and either raises your vibration or lowers it. As a seeker of transformation, it's crucial to take responsibility for aligning yourself with higher vibrational energy. This involves mindful attention to everything you consume, both physically and mentally. For instance, consuming plant-based foods and avoiding harmful substances like alcohol and drugs raises your vibration. Similarly, consuming positive and uplifting content, like spiritual literature, meditative music, and inspiring biographies, can help you maintain positive energy throughout your day.

By prioritizing your spiritual practice and aligning your lifestyle to support it, you will be able to accelerate your evolution and experience higher states of consciousness.

Create a Night and Morning Routine

Establishing an effective daily routine is important for sustained spiritual growth. The two most important routines are your night and morning rituals.

Your nightly routine directly influences the quality of your sleep, which in turn affects your energy and clarity throughout the day. Ayurveda, the yoga of health, recommends that you go to sleep by 10:00 p.m. to allow the natural cycle of rest to start. Dedicate an hour to wind down before bed. Engage in activities that help you relax, like reading or listening to calm music.

Equally vital is an empowering morning routine because the way you begin your morning sets the tone for the day. Consider incorporating these suggestions:

1. Upon waking up, set an intention to radiate positive energy throughout the day. (For example, say the affirmation: *Today, I will channel positive energy and bring love and light to all aspects of my experience.*)

2. Meditate.

3. Begin your day with a purposeful, spiritually uplifting activity, such as reading inspiring text or practicing mindful movement.

Food

Food possesses both physical and spiritual qualities. Fresh, natural, and light foods are imbued with high spiritual energy, often referred to as *prana* or *chi*. It's important to avoid overeating, particularly at dinner, as digestion diverts vital energy that could otherwise be directed toward spiritual growth.

Food provides nourishment not only for your physical body but also for your energy body. There are some foods you should avoid because they lower your vibration. These fall into three categories:

1. **Meat.** Eating animals is detrimental to both physical health and spiritual advancement. The more evolved an animal is, the more energetically toxic its meat is for humans. You can transition away from meat in phases: first, eliminate mammals (beef, pork); then poultry (chicken, turkey); and finally, fish. We will explore food in greater depth in Step 6.

2. **Intoxicants.** Alcohol and other psychoactive drugs lower your vibration. Unfortunately, alcohol has become a common feature of our social life due to ceaseless advertising

from alcohol manufacturers. Make a conscious choice to stop purchasing alcoholic beverages and opt for non-alcoholic alternatives in social gatherings.

3. **Processed Foods.** These foods lack nutrition and are laden with chemicals for preservation. These are detrimental to your physical and energetic body. Prioritize fresh, whole foods instead.

The increase in veganism and vegetarianism reflects a collective shift toward higher spiritual and ethical values. As individuals become more spiritually aware, they begin to recognize the interconnectedness of all things and seek ways to live in harmony with the natural world. This includes mindful dietary choices that consider the environment, animal welfare, and personal well-being.

Information

What you read, watch, and listen to influences your state of mind and your consciousness. To nurture your mind, actively seek out books, lectures, and teachings by individuals who embody higher consciousness and are committed to uplifting humanity. Conversely, avoid consuming content from mass media, which profits by inducing people into negative states, such as fear, powerlessness, and agitation.

People

Surround yourself with those committed to cultivating higher consciousness. Limit spending time with people who radiate lower vibrations (fear, anger, greed, powerlessness, lack of purpose, and addictions). But avoid the trap of superiority; this isn't about judging others but about aligning with the energy that nurtures your growth.

Physical Exercise

The body is a temple of consciousness and needs to be honored. Physical activities move energy, leading to balance and harmony. Practices such as yoga, tai chi, and qi gong are excellent ways to promote physical vitality and spiritual expansion. Mindful breathing and movement also reduce stress, anxiety, and heaviness.

Even simple walks in nature—through forests, parks, or open skies—reconnect you with universal flow. The mind clears, the spirit renews, and the truth reveals itself: you are not separate but woven into the living wholeness of all things.

EXERCISE
Support Your Spiritual Practice

1. Design your pre-sleep ritual. Choose a set of activities for winding down before sleep and schedule them on your calendar.

2. Design your morning ritual of setting an intention, meditating, and doing spiritual practice.

JOANNA'S JOURNEY

Joanna's story shows how the spiritual journey can be a winding path with many stops. Sometimes, it is through loss of faith that we open ourselves to spiritual rebirth.

The spiritual journey is the process of rediscovering our essence. It involves cultivating self-knowledge and claiming who we truly are, stripped of social and cultural conditioning. You will likely encounter many dead ends and false starts along the way. The search for my authentic self has taken me from fundamental Christianity to militant atheism, from Sunday school to the gentlemen's club, and places in between.

I was born in Tondo, a slum in Manila, Philippines. Though my large family was impoverished and lacked the most basic amenities, I felt content growing up in a cramped but love-filled home. At six years old, with the dream of a better life, my mother loaded me onto a plane to be the first to join my dad, who was already in America. But the dream turned into a nightmare. My father was a clinically narcissistic and abusive man, in whose shadow I lost my natural joy. The journey back to that spiritual place of childlike optimism and wonder has been a harrowing one.

Outwardly, my father played the part of a pious man. He was critical of everything outside the confines of the church, and living under that constraint, I grew close to the kids from my church as if they were family. Being a passionate person, I immersed myself in fundamentalist Christianity through activism in youth groups. As I grew older, however, I began examining the world around me and grew loathsome of the hypocrisy I was experiencing.

When I graduated from high school, my dad refused to pay for my college. Determined to receive an education, I joined the United States military and served in the army for three years before beginning my undergraduate studies at Santa Barbara City College. This was my first experience of intellectual and spiritual freedom, and so began my process of stripping away, in both a figurative and literal sense, the beliefs and insecurities that no longer served me. I began reading and taking classes in theology, learning about the gospel of Judas and the Gnostic gospels that hadn't quite made it into the Bible. I was dumbfounded to learn the "Word of God" was a compilation of books cherry-picked to become a tool of control.

As I gradually outgrew religion, I became free of the fear of judgment from the "godly" people who had conditioned my life. In 2006, at 26, I moved to California and began stripping in a nightclub to support myself through college. During this time, I met my ex-husband, who was an atheist. Although I was initially hesitant to reject divinity altogether, the works of Christopher Hitchens and my husband's support eventually persuaded me. I channeled the anger I had at my religious upbringing and became a militant atheist.

Professionally, I had aspired to become an English teacher and help struggling teens, à la LouAnne Johnson from *Dangerous Minds,* but by the time I received my master's degree in teaching, I found the California school system unviable for a long-term future. I switched to the non-profit sector in 2011 and to the corporate world in 2015. During those years, I was never able to find the right fit. That's why a part of me was relieved to be laid off during the pandemic of 2020.

Unemployed and divorced, with copious amounts of free time, I wondered what was next for me. By this time, I had, thankfully, mellowed from a militant atheist to a more laid-back, regular one. I decided to use this time to learn more about the universe, perhaps as an unconscious way to confirm my atheism. I immediately felt drawn to the study of black holes. I would eventually recognize that my interest being piqued in this way had been a divine nudge, but at the time, I was simply curious. I started watching the World Science Festival videos on YouTube. This endeavor to understand the cosmos would eventually transform me spiritually in a way I could never have imagined. As I listened to the greatest scientists discuss how the universe works, I was amazed that the best and brightest minds in science were unsure of the true nature of reality. How, then, could I be so certain of my own beliefs? Further, the exploration of science had a mystical aspect, with concepts such as the holographic principle. It seems the only thing we can be sure of is that everything is connected.

The lockdown of 2020 became a frenzy of reading and absorbing material to understand this connectedness. I began exploring spiritual practices, such as meditation, to go within. Eventually, I got to a state where I would meditate for hours.

In 2021, my search for spirituality without religion eventually led me to Children of Infinity. Determined to not return to the corporate world, I embraced this pivotal time of spiritual discovery and development. I participated in an 8-month book study program and was transformed. Among the many great works I read was the book *Living the Law of One*, based on the Ra material. This became my new bible, tying together with an ornate bow all the pieces I had collected over a lifetime.

Having spent so much time as a spiritual glutton, I now found myself digesting all I had consumed during my spiritual search. I was so inspired by the Ra material that I contacted L/L Research in hopes that I could be of service there. In 2022, I started working with L/L, which allows me to serve others on the path while supporting myself spiritually. I feel blessed to work in an environment lacking in office politics—focusing instead on honesty, love, and caring.

I want to encourage people to listen to their hearts and to be courageous. Our inner wisdom can guide us to our highest life, but we must first be true to ourselves.

Joanna Burns works at L/L Research, a spiritual organization dedicated to sharing information to aid in the spiritual evolution of humankind. L/L is home to the Ra material, an advanced metaphysical work.

Step 6: Align with Soul Purpose

"For success, like happiness, cannot be pursued; it must ensue, and it only does so as the unintended side effect of one's personal dedication to a cause greater than oneself."

—Victor Frankl

"The mystery of human existence lies not in just staying alive, but in finding something to live for."

—Fyodor Dostoyevsky

According to pre-birth planning research, we incarnate in physical reality to cultivate gifts that have been acquired over lifetimes. These gifts may include artistic expression, healing, leadership, or the ability to raise consciousness. These gifts do not typically come fully developed—they are like seeds you grow and cultivate over time.

Once we incarnate, however, we forget the plan and lose track of our connection to the divine. Instead, we fall victim to the deep-rooted programming we are born into.

In the unenlightened state, we become hamsters running on the wheel of conditioned goals, following *the way of the tribe*, a set of rules that ensure survival and progress in a tribal system but do not align with what our hearts truly desire. The way of the tribe in the Western world today includes getting a good education, finding a well-paying job, getting married, having children, and then retiring one day, hopefully with a substantial 401(k).

Caught amidst the striving for material success, we work hard, trade our lives for money, and consume like there is no tomorrow. But the effort only feeds the never-ending cycle of desire and dissatisfaction. We become trapped in the rat race, always chasing the next promotion, the bigger house, the fancier car. Depression, anxiety, and suicidal thoughts are common among people stuck in this cycle. We are driven to be more productive, efficient, and successful—but at what cost? We sacrifice well-being, relationships, and happiness in the pursuit of material wealth. The tragedy is that we also lose our individuality to become just like everyone else.

Following the way of the tribe does not bring happiness, merely exhaustion. The truth is that material wealth and possessions cannot provide the true sense of fulfillment we crave. As spiritual beings, we need more than survival and security: we need a higher purpose for being.

The deepest part of our being yearns to operate at higher consciousness, to tap into the realms of knowledge, wisdom, transformation, love, and joy. The journey requires the courage to honor our individuality.

Think of Earth as a huge orchestra in which every instrument plays its own unique part. Even if it's not audible to everyone else, each person's contribution matters to the harmony of the whole. If the piano tried to sound like a violin, the whole orchestra would lose its function and purpose. You have to honor your uniqueness because, metaphysically, your soul purpose is a unique expression of Source's creativity. Unless you honor your uniqueness, you cannot find fulfillment.

The Twelve Archetypes

A simple way to understand your gifts is to study archetypes—symbolic patterns shared universally across cultures. When you resonate with a particular archetype, you understand your inspirations and values, and the general direction needed to express it. Here are the twelve primary archetypes derived from the works of spiritual teachers Carolyn Myss and Ainslie MacLeod:

1. *The Teacher Archetype* values personal growth and finds fulfillment in helping others learn and develop.

2. *The Healer Archetype* values empathy and compassion and finds fulfillment in helping others restore themselves to wholeness, peace, and balance. It focuses on healing, whether physical, emotional, psychological, or spiritual.

3. *The Leader Archetype* values vision and clarity and finds fulfillment in leading others toward a common goal. It is characterized by a strong sense of direction and a desire to inspire.

4. *The Visionary Archetype* values creativity and imagination and finds fulfillment in inspiring others to think outside the box and pursue their dreams. It is about breaking free from limiting beliefs and old thought patterns that no longer serve us.

5. *The Caregiver Archetype* values empathy and kindness and finds fulfillment in caring for children, the elderly, animals, or anyone needing compassion and support.

6. *The Explorer Archetype* values curiosity and discovery and finds fulfillment in traveling, learning new things, and pushing the boundaries of what is known. It is characterized by a sense of adventure and a desire to explore new horizons.

7. ***The Inventor Archetype*** values creativity and resourcefulness and finds fulfillment in inventing new technologies or products. It focuses on creating new things and solving problems through innovation.

8. ***The Thinker Archetype*** values intelligence and wisdom and finds fulfillment in studying philosophy, science, and other intellectual subjects. It loves analyzing and understanding complex concepts and systems.

9. ***The Creative Archetype*** values imagination and intuition and finds fulfillment in writing, painting, music, and other forms of artistic expression. It is characterized by a desire to create beautiful things.

10. ***The Performer Archetype*** values charisma and charm and finds fulfillment in acting, singing, dancing, and other forms of performance art. It is about entertaining and captivating others.

11. ***The Sage Archetype*** values knowledge and insight and finds fulfillment in mentoring others, providing advice and guidance, and simply sharing life experiences. It focuses on imparting wisdom and guidance to others.

12. ***The Mystic Archetype*** values intuition and mystical experiences and finds fulfillment in pursuing spiritual practices, exploring higher states of consciousness, and making them accessible to others. It is characterized by spiritual depth and an ability to connect to the non-physical dimension.

Multiple archetypes may be activated in an incarnation. For example, my journey includes the archetypes of mystic, teacher, and leader. Most people can easily identify three to six archetypes that characterize their human journey.

EXERCISE
Work with Your Archetype

- List at least three primary archetypes that resonate with you.
- How can you use your specific archetypes to guide your journey?

The Partnership Dysfunction: Misalignment

One's relationship with the universe, just like any partnership, can become dysfunctional. This happens when the physical self becomes so entangled in material existence that it cannot hear the guidance of the Higher Self and becomes *spiritually deaf*. The primary causes of spiritual deafness are strongly rooted states of powerlessness, victimhood, and fear. Another common reason is the all-consuming greed for power. When accumulating power becomes the sole focus of an incarnation, its spiritual purpose is lost. Spiritually deaf people do not understand their reason for being on the planet and create misery for themselves and others.

The good news is that the universe can help snap you out when you get lost. These interventions usually come in the form of crises, which are actually opportunities to refocus your life. For example, a sudden health or relationship crisis may show up to help you focus on what matters. When a crisis shows up, it is time to slow down, recognize its gift, and refocus your attention on your spiritual purpose.

Your Soul Purpose and the Stages of Life

Your soul purpose is not only unique to you—it is also unique to your stage of life. As we evolve during an incarnation, each stage requires a different understanding and spiritual practice. What worked for you in your 20s may not be appropriate in your forties. For example, in our twenties, many of us are *spiritual militants* who consider it our sacred duty to save others by forcing our views onto them. In our forties, however, we may realize the futility of force and seek a more compassionate approach. It is critical to understand that your cultural model of life progression may not be in alignment with your soul purpose.

Stages of Life: The Conditioned Path

When we examine the lifecycle of a modern human being, we observe three broad stages: schooling, employment and relationships, and retirement. These phases, unfortunately, are influenced by a larger narrative: consumerism.

The first stage—schooling—takes up roughly a quarter of our lives. Its goal is to produce workers who can create economic value, rather than outstanding human beings who can elevate humanity. The focus on economic value leaves little time for learning about our true nature and how to serve.

Built upon a spiritually denuded foundation, the next stage—employment and relationships—becomes a complex struggle. We work to achieve economic flexibility but then spend our hard-earned money on endless consumption. Our partners have also been trained to be consumers, which means that seeking happiness through accumulation now becomes a family pursuit. As we approach this stage's midpoint, we may undergo a midlife crisis—a time of inner turmoil where we face questions about our identity, life choices, and mortality. If we have grown in awareness, we begin to see beyond the cultural conditioning and ask questions about the pathway to true happiness. The search for answers can lead to a spiritual awakening as our Higher Self and the universe try to nudge us toward our higher purpose for being on this planet.

The third stage—retirement—can be the worst phase because consumerism keeps pointing us away from the reality of mortality. Many in this phase are programmed to want to feel and look younger, which they seek through plastic surgery, expensive cars, property ownership, and finding younger partners.

Stages of Life: The Path of Spiritual Purpose

Is there a better way of living than the conditioned path? There is.

The Ashrama system, which originated during the Vedic Period in India, offers a model of living aligned with the natural progression of life energy.

As we age, our physical vitality decreases while our wisdom grows. Cognizant of the progression, the Ashrama system divides life into four quarters, with each stage having its own purpose and focus.

The first quarter, known as *Brahmacharya*, is a time of learning and growth under the guidance of spiritual masters. During this phase, which is typically below the age of twenty, the focus is on education and discovering your purpose in life.

The second quarter, *Grihastha*, translates as "one situated in family life." This phase, typically falling between ages twenty and forty, is a time of exploration, self-discovery, and gathering wisdom. The focus is learning to love and care for family members and to nourish yourself and those closest to you.

The third phase, *Vanaprastha*, marks a natural evolution from serving a smaller family to a larger one. During this phase, which typically occurs between the ages of forty and sixty, the focus is on using one's wisdom to serve the greater good. In this phase, one may teach, devote oneself to spiritual practices, and acquire more wisdom.

The last phase, *Sannyasa,* is a time of renunciation. During this phase, typically at age sixty or older, one minimizes worldly responsibilities and focuses solely on enlightenment. The focus is on spiritual work and practices, letting go of distractions, and making every day count.

One of the great takeaways from the Ashrama system is that your purpose is different based on your stage of life. By aligning with this natural progression, you can live a more purposeful and fulfilled life.

How to Clarify Your Life Purpose

Your life purpose lies at the intersection of three opportunities:

1. **Joy.** Certain activities or experiences light you up and make you feel fulfilled. These activities, being aligned with the source of joy within, indicate your true purpose in life.

2. **Gifts.** You possess unique skills and talents. What have you learned through experience that you can use to serve others? These are your "gifts." Sharing them will make you a source of light.

3. **Inspiration.** What inspires you? What challenges and growth opportunities excite you? Pursuing what inspires you deepens your connection to your Higher Self.

EXERCISE
Clarify Your Life Purpose

Answer the following questions by writing down the first thought that comes to your mind. Don't censor or edit your thoughts. That will help you express your authentic self.

1. If you had no external factors to consider, such as money or recognition, what would you do just for the sheer joy of it?

2. What gifts and skills have you acquired throughout your life? These could include challenges you have overcome, lessons you have learned, or skills you have developed. Don't worry about how valuable your gifts might be to others or whether they're popular.

3. What inspires you? What do you think would be a worthwhile challenge? Choose what you feel connected to and passionate about. Choose neither something so trivial that it requires no stretching, nor something so overwhelming that it paralyzes you.

4. Once you have answered the previous three questions, combine your joy, gifts, and opportunities for growth into a single idea that represents your life purpose.

5. Consider how you can best serve your purpose at this stage of your life. What skills or knowledge do you need to acquire to continue making progress? For example, if you want to learn how to play piano, you may find a teacher and take online courses. Or if you want to be a writer, you can improve your skills through daily reading and writing. What is the smallest daily commitment you can make serve your purpose?

Misconceptions About Life Purpose

There are three major misconceptions about life purpose.

First, many people believe that their life purpose is a concrete place to be reached. In reality, not only is it not a place, it is not even a concrete path but rather a theme used to create your path. You have the creative freedom to express your life purpose in any way that brings you joy. For example, if you want to heal others, you can learn about traditional medicine, therapy, shamanism, or healing through dance. Instead of being attached to one specific way of pursuing your life purpose, build the path that will create joy for you.

The second misconception is that once you begin following your life purpose, all your problems will suddenly disappear: you will become financially secure, healthy, loved, and admired. The idea that everything will be perfect once you arrive at a certain place is a fairytale ending. In reality, growth occurs in response to resistance. A lack of problems is not a measure of spiritual growth—it is more likely a measure of spiritual stagnation. The most important lessons of an incarnation are learned by dealing with the most complex issues. As you progress spiritually, you will get opportunities to master more complex lessons, just like progressing through grades in school.

The third misconception is that your life purpose is static and unchanging. In reality, your life purpose changes and evolves with your abilities. It is important to remain open to new experiences and opportunities, which will help you continually reevaluate and refine your purpose based on how you can serve in the highest way.

Obstacles to Living Your Life Purpose

Here are the four most common types of obstacles you may face in the pursuit of your higher purpose and how to overcome them:

1. **Insufficient Clarity.** Clarity about your life purpose helps you make decisions. For example, should you accept more money at the expense of time needed for inner growth? If you had clarity, you would not hesitate to decline the opportunity. But for those who lack clarity, making any kind of choice—big or small—can be overwhelming.

   To gain clarity, devote time weekly to candidly reflect on how your life aligns with your purpose. Ask yourself, "How well am I moving in the direction of my purpose? Is there anything that does not contribute to it that I can eliminate?"

2. **Procrastination.** The most common difficulty people face is getting started. Often, there are psychological blocks that underlie procrastination, such as fear of failure or the unknown, lack of belief in oneself, or stress arising from too many options. Instead of being overwhelmed, break big tasks into manageable steps, and then stick to these small, daily steps until they become automatic. When one habit is firmly established, stretch by including more complex practices. Avoid overthinking and staying within your comfort zone—while it can provide feelings of security and stability, it hinders growth.

3. **Attachment to specific results.** When you insist on a certain outcome, you limit the possibilities the universe can bring to you. For example, you might envision working toward your soul purpose of helping others become healthier by writing best-selling books. Yet, if you insist this is the only way to

your purpose, you will miss out on other possibilities, such as sharing your wisdom through podcasts, videos, or group teachings.

Insistence on specific results is often driven by the ego rather than a higher motive. If you probe deeper, you might find that your desire to become a best-selling author is driven by your admiration for another author's life. But what if you have a different path? The key is to trust your own path and offer yourself to the great dance of life. To avoid attachment to specific results, focus on the *essence* of your work rather than on a specific *outcome*. Allow the universe and your Higher Self to open doors for you by exploring all possible pathways and trusting the process.

4. **Losing momentum.** The most important facilitator of progress is momentum. It takes significant effort to create spiritual momentum, and if you're not vigilant, it is very easy to lose it. Here are the most common causes:

   a. **Distractions.** Distractions disrupt your focus and sidetrack you with low-value activities. For example, you might be cultivating a writing practice by consistently producing five hundred words a day. One day, however, a friend tells you about a popular Netflix series, and you decide to check out an episode. Four hours later, you're still caught up in the drama. The next day, you wake up groggy and can't muster the mental energy to focus on your practice. If such disruptions repeat, you will lose confidence in your ability to sustain your practice, and eventually, you'll quit the practice. To avoid distractions, eliminate their sources (see Step 2 on removing distractions) and maintain vigilance.

b. **Discouragement.** If you feel results are not coming quickly enough, you might lose motivation. While it is normal in our fast-food culture to expect quick results, that is not how life works. Just as a seed takes time to grow, it also takes time for intention and effort to mature into results. You can avoid discouragement by refocusing on your vision and avoiding unrealistic expectations. Be willing to invest the necessary time, energy, and resources to make your vision a reality.

It also might be difficult to stay motivated if you live in an unsupportive environment with toxic family members or friends. But you are not meant to be stuck with toxic people. Change your environment and surround yourself with like-minded people who support your purpose and offer guidance, encouragement, and accountability.

c. **Burnout.** Burnout is a state of emotional and physical exhaustion caused by prolonged stress, overwork, and excessive demands. Spiritual burnout occurs when you try too hard. Living your purpose requires allowing the universe to do its part and trusting its timing. Pushing arises from the ego's need for self-validation; it is not the same as inspired persistence, which arises from your Higher Self. To prevent burnout, practice focusing on frequent rejuvenation and sustainable effort rather than ceaseless activity.

You can avoid these obstacles by staying vigilant and following routines that support your commitment to your life purpose.

EXERCISE
Avoid Obstacles to Living Your Life Purpose

Write down your answers to the following questions:

1. Are you clear about your life purpose? What trade-offs must you make to honor it?

2. How can you build and sustain spiritual momentum? The steps might include having daily and monthly goals, devoting time to structured learning, such as interactive courses, and working with peers who keep you accountable. Experiment to find what works best for you.

3. State your goals in ways that avoid attachment to narrow paths. For example, instead of writing, "I want to become a bestselling author," write, "I want to serve every person who can benefit from my knowledge. I will explore all possible channels to find what works best for me."

4. It is not *if* you will face discouragement but *when*. Living your highest life requires living outside your comfort zone, which is difficult. The best way to handle discouragement is to prepare for it in advance. What steps will you take when you feel discouraged? Examples include writing in your journal, talking to your mentor, or taking time off to rejuvenate.

DANIEL'S JOURNEY

Spiritual transformation is a life-long process leading to the fulfillment of one's soul purpose. Daniel recounts how he built his spiritual self, often having to rip out and replace the ideas and beliefs that no longer suited his purpose.

I see the process of spiritual transformation as building a beautiful temple—it is a lengthy and meticulous undertaking. The bricks in this structure are beliefs, and finding the correct bricks can take years of study and reflection. For me, the process started early in life.

Being on the spiritual path for so long, I now believe that I chose my life path during pre-birth planning. I painstakingly chose my physical, emotional, and intellectual attributes like a child designing his avatar in a video game, selecting the characteristics best suited for the goals I set for myself in my life to come.

I kind of sneaked in as an unwanted pregnancy to get my biological family's genes and then moved into the waiting arms of my adopted parents, who provided me with the support needed to cultivate my thinking. My birth mother wished for me to be raised Catholic, and my adoptive mother acquiesced to this wish. She died in my eighth-grade year, followed shortly after by the passing of my adoptive father. It was excruciating losing them, but being on my own offered me the freedom to thread together a life of independent thought.

I became an avid reader of everything from science to the supernatural. The numerous beliefs I encountered began to form the foundational bricks of my worldview. My first task was to discard the bricks from my Catholic faith to make way for new spiritual ideas. Many of the rules and beliefs by which I was raised seemed arbitrary. For example, why would a baby need baptism when Christ has already paid the price of original sin? Surely, newborns have nothing from which to be washed clean. Fairly soon, even though I was surrounded by religion, I became spiritually independent.

At age thirteen, I started looking into superstition. Though I give no credence to throwing salt over one's shoulder, knocking on wood, or wearing unwashed socks to play baseball, understanding confirmation bias was a critical brick. From then on, I became a conscious optimist, focusing on the positive in the world. At age fourteen, around the time of my mother's death, the book *Seth Speaks* struck a nerve that reverberated through my soul. It was this line of study that opened my eyes to the broader spiritual reality that we are multidimensional beings, not limited humans. I went on to add the shamanic perspective of Carlos Castaneda to my growing spiritual repertoire as well. I even dabbled in psychedelics but feared my journey to the edge would result in falling off of it, so I abandoned that path.

My voracious appetite for books led me to science and engineering. I received a computer engineering degree from Boston University. The two highest-paying jobs I could get were in defense and finance. I chose finance over defense, despite the lesser pay, as I found the idea of building weapons appalling. I worked a few years for an employer, rising through the ranks and diving deeper into the world of software.

Soon, my independent streak led me to start my own ventures—something I have done for decades now. Some of these did quite well and were sold to companies such as Dell and PNC Bank. I began integrating what I learned through business, science, and spirituality into my everyday life, collecting and replacing more bricks as my understanding progressed.

The banking crisis of 2007 offered me some free time from my busy life, and I found a key brick through the works of Bashar in 2008. I had spent my life comparing things to find what was correct when no such comparison was necessary. I began to see the universe as inclusive rather than exclusive, in that *this* and *that* can be equally true. *This* may be true for me while *that* is true for you. This realization put me on a metaphysical path where I could create my reality directly, rather than through attitude alone. I spent the next few years consuming everything Bashar offered, thus forming the final brick of my spiritual foundation. At last, I was ready to build upon the foundation.

I gave myself permission to graduate from student to teacher in 2011 by launching a community on WhatsApp called Oneness Circle. Working with people in small groups brought me great joy. I've since added hypnosis and past life regression to my repertoire of skills. I find people (or rather, they find me) who, though deeply spiritual, are often confused about the world at large. I tell them they don't have to know all the answers—they need only collect bricks of truth to add to their spiritual foundation, and maintain the humility required to remove any beliefs that hinder truth-seeking. I lean heavily on the spiritual teachings and teachers that came before me, including the Tao Te Ching, Brian Weiss, Edgar Cayce, and many more.

In Carol Pearson's book *The Hero Within* she describes the six archetypes of spiritual development, stating that we must begin and end our development with the innocence of a child. Helping others has been key to my transformation, awakening my spiritual self, and rediscovering that childlike innocence. Indeed, Pearson's archetypes confirm Bashar's teaching that two contradictory truths need not be mutually exclusive—such as the knowledge of a scholar partnered with a childlike altruism.

I found Children of Infinity as soon as it launched in 2020 and immediately felt I was meant to be a part of the work being done there. I strive toward becoming a one hundred percent spiritual being within my earthly body, leaving my human reactive being behind, though I'm unsure such complete enlightenment is possible. Through continued teaching and learning, I hope to bring light to others.

Daniel Endy has retired from a successful career in high-tech startups. He donates his time to serving spiritual organizations such as the International Association for Near-Death Studies (IANDS) and Children of Infinity.

Step 7: Grow and Take Risks

"Growth is never by mere chance; it is the result of forces working together."

—James Cash Penney

"The lotus is the most beautiful flower, whose petals open one by one. But it will only grow in the mud. In order to grow and gain wisdom, first you must have the mud—the obstacles of life and its suffering. The mud speaks of the common ground that humans share, no matter what our stations in life... Whether we have it all or we have nothing, we are all faced with the same obstacles: sadness, loss, illness, dying and death. If we are to strive as human beings to gain more wisdom, more kindness and more compassion, we must have the intention to grow as a lotus and open each petal one by one."

—Goldie Hawn

Reaching your full potential isn't accidental; it's the result of an *intentional process of lifelong improvement*. The journey involves cultivating self-awareness, acquiring knowledge and skills, improving your mindset, and navigating the inevitable challenges of growth. This may sound overwhelming, especially if you are new to the growth journey. This chapter will simplify the process by breaking it down into actionable steps, helping you cultivate a growth mindset and apply a structured approach to continuous improvement.

Growth and the Human Journey

The most remarkable gift we possess is our ability to learn. No matter our age, our brains are designed to adapt, rewire, and forge new pathways—a phenomenon known as neuroplasticity. As children, we learn effortlessly because we are driven by curiosity and wonder. Yet as adults, we often limit learning to necessity, acquiring new skills only when external demands force us to. What a wasted opportunity!

Growth fulfills the innate human need for intellectual expansion. If you think of everything you've learned since birth—whether small feats like learning to use email, or big accomplishments like cultivating relationships, raising children, or building businesses—each experience has expanded your understanding of yourself and the world. By achieving mastery as an artist, a healer, a teacher, or an innovator, your growth contributes to the collective unfolding of human potential.

Why, then, do we so often resist growth? The reason is that growth requires *change*, which our biology is hardwired to resist. Over millions of years of evolution, the human brain has learned that change can lead to danger. Some of our ancestors who veered off the well-trodden path were eaten by saber-toothed tigers or poisoned by eating unfamiliar fruit. Although such dangers don't exist in modern societies, our brains still react to change with caution, preferring comfort over the mental effort required to adapt. As a result, many only grow when forced by circumstance, missing the chance to evolve intentionally.

The path of *unconscious* growth (learning passively from one's own experience) is slow. As Benjamin Franklin said, "Experience keeps a dear school, yet fools will learn in no other."

But we don't have to grow at a snail's pace. Instead, we can accelerate our development by choosing growth deliberately, by identifying key areas for improvement, dedicating time and energy to learning, and seeking guidance from those who have already walked the path.

Adopting a systematic growth process can transform your life, just as it transformed mine when I encountered John Maxwell's teachings in 2004. From him, I learned the importance of *having a concrete plan for growth*. Inspired by his guidance, I implemented two simple but powerful habits: dedicating one hour daily to reading and turning mundane chores into learning opportunities by listening to audiobooks.

In the two decades since then, I have read five hundred books and listened to two hundred audio programs, which has enabled me to master crucial life skills: time and money management, investing, being effective with people, content design, leadership, and growing Children of Infinity. These skills have enriched my life and equipped me to serve others.

Fixed vs. Growth Mindset

Many of us do not pursue conscious growth because of one crippling assumption: *"I can't learn."* To break free from this self-limiting belief, let's dive into the groundbreaking psychological research by Dr. Carol Dweck. Her research reveals that people adopt one of two mindsets about growth: the fixed mindset and the growth mindset.

Those with a fixed mindset believe in *inherent talent*—that they are either good at something or they are not. They further believe that if they are not good at something, there is little they can do to improve. This sets up a vicious cycle: You believe you can't learn, and so, you don't.

People with a growth mindset believe that through practice and repetition, anything can be mastered. Since they believe in their capacity to learn, they exhibit greater resilience, creativity, and willingness to take risks, resulting in higher levels of achievement than those with fixed mindsets.

If you're ready to unlock your highest potential, the first step is clear: You must cultivate the growth mindset. Your mindset isn't just a trait; it's a decision. And that decision shapes your future.

EXERCISE
Examine Your Beliefs About Growth

Let's examine your beliefs about growth. Write answers to the following questions:

1. What beliefs about growth limit you? These might include beliefs such as *I am too old, too busy, not a quick learner, not smart,* or *not good with numbers*.

2. How did you acquire these beliefs? These limiting notions might have been passed on to you through family, authority figures, or media programming. They might also result from experiences that led you to doubt your ability (for example, I remember my art teacher telling me I had no talent for art). The point is, these beliefs are not innate: since you *acquired* them, you can *discard* them.

3. What beliefs will empower you and assist your growth? These are beliefs such as:

    I can learn anything I want to.

    The brain is flexible and can learn at any age.

How to Implement a Process of Intentional Growth

An effective process of improvement requires systematic planning, execution, evaluation, and adjustment. To implement the growth process, follow these four steps:

Step 1. Choose an area of focus.

When people begin the growth journey, their tendency is to want to overhaul their entire lives overnight. This "fix everything at once" approach is precisely what sets them up for failure. Why? Because the human brain has a limited capacity for cognitively demanding tasks, and nothing taxes the brain more than change.

Instead of aiming for a total makeover, focus on one area for the next three to six months. Choose an area that you believe can make the biggest difference in your life. There are two easy ways to select this area:

1. Examine the major areas of your life and select the one that needs the most growth, for example, health, work, relationships, finances, or contribution.

2. Use the Twelve Soul Archetypes discussed in the previous step to guide your focus.

Step 2. Implement a weekly growth cycle.

The weekly cycle, which creates the foundation of growth, consists of three phases: learning, applying, and adjusting.

LEARNING

To make major strides in your focus area, what knowledge and skills do you need to master?

For example, if your focus is health, the key areas to master are nutrition, exercise, and stress management. The specific skills may include cooking nutritious, easy-to-prepare meals; meditating; and managing time to focus on exercise and self-care.

After selecting skills, the next step is to choose the most effective resources to help you learn quickly. If you're a beginner, you can learn from books and audiobooks from experts. At the intermediate level, you can work directly with teachers. This requires a greater investment of money, but a good teacher can save you years of effort. Finally, at the advanced level, it is best to work one-on-one with mentors, people who are already where you want to be and are willing to guide you.

Once you have identified the skills you need to cultivate and the resources that will help you cultivate them, it is time to create a weekly plan for learning. The plan should address *what, how,* and *when.* Consider these examples:

- For next week, what do you want to learn?
  I want to learn how to have more joy.

- How will you learn?
  I will learn from the book Living with Joy *by Sanaya Roman.*

- When will you learn?
  Every day at 9 p.m. for thirty minutes, just before going to bed.

- What are the next action steps to implement your learning plan and achieve that goal?
  - *Buy the book*
  - *Set a daily phone notification to read at 9 p.m.*

APPLYING

The second phase in the learning cycle is to apply what you have learned. Remember, the goal of learning is action, not merely knowledge. Learning serves no purpose if it is not applied. Ask yourself:

1. *What have I learned?* When reading a book, take a few minutes after each chapter to write down what you have learned.

2. *How can I apply what I have learned?* Do I need to cultivate a specific practice? Adopt a new belief system? What exactly are the changes I need to make?

3. *To apply what I have learned, what daily and weekly activities are needed?* For example, if the book you are reading recommends creating a gratitude practice, you might commit to writing a sentence of gratitude every day in a journal.

ADJUSTING

The third phase in the growth cycle is adjusting. Examine your growth cycle on a weekly basis and make any changes needed. Here are the questions to drive this process:

1. What is working? What is not working?

2. What should I do more? What should I do less?

3. What should I start doing? What should I stop doing?

To maintain momentum, devote thirty to sixty minutes each week to focused reviewing and planning. Critically examine the last week and identify what you can improve. Then set goals for the next week to apply what you have learned.

Remember that *change takes time*. That's why it is important to commit to your focus area for at least three months. By reviewing the growth cycle weekly, you will notice improvements and create victories.

After three months, ask yourself if you have made sufficient progress in this area. If you have, choose another area of focus. Otherwise, devote three more months to the current focus area.

The discipline of devoting at least a quarter of the year to one area will help you stay focused and create massive growth over time.

Step 3. Invest in your growth.

Growth requires investing in yourself. To experience lifelong growth, make two commitments:

1. Invest at least an hour a day to learn, plan, and reflect.

2. Invest three to five percent of your income in growth. Use the money to buy educational materials, attend workshops, and learn from experts. Additionally, reinvest ten percent of pay raises in yourself.

There is a profound principle at work when you consistently invest: due to the *law of compounding,* even seemingly small actions, when repeated daily, create monumental change. Essentially, your daily choices, compounded over time, *become your destiny.*

Consider the oft-quoted example: Would you rather have a penny doubled every day for thirty days or $100,000 today? A penny doubled every day seems like a tiny amount of money, and indeed, it is a tiny sum for most of the thirty days. If you calculate the growth, after ten days, you have a meagre $5. After twenty days, you have $5000, which is still small compared to $100,000.

The magic of compounding becomes obvious on Day 25, when the amount crosses $100,000. On Day 28, it is more than $1,000,000, and on Day 30, it becomes more than $5,000,000. Compounding works the same way with personal and spiritual growth—dedicating daily time to your growth can profoundly change your life.

EXERCISE
Dedicate Resources to Growth

1. How much time do you commit to growing daily? Schedule the time in your calendar.

2. How much money do you commit monthly to your growth? Set this amount aside.

3. Research books, online courses, and workshops that will help you grow.

Step 4: Take necessary risks.

To reach our potential, we must risk venturing out of our comfort zone. Yet, fear—that powerful trickster of the mind—keeps many trapped in unfulfilling careers, stagnant relationships, and lives of quiet resignation.

Fear distorts reality and creates illusions of the worst possible outcomes. In psychology, this is called *catastrophizing*, which turns ordinary risks into mental monsters. The mind chatter can go something like this:

> *"I hate my job and would rather turn my hobby into a profession. But, if I quit now to start my own business, I will lose the health benefits, which I really need. The economy is not doing good, so I won't be able to pay rent. I will run out of my savings in six months, after which I will lose everything and be homeless for the rest of my life."*

It's no wonder the debilitating voice imprisons us.

The way to stop catastrophizing is to critically examine the all-or-nothing approach to risk. Taking risks doesn't require abandoning prudence—the point is to take *calculated risks,* not senseless ones.

For a risk to be "calculated," you first need to thoroughly do your research. During the research phase, you might find opportunities that require risking nothing more than sweat equity (the hours you don't get paid for). It is always possible to begin by taking small steps in the right direction, which will help you develop your risk tolerance.

Let's say you are unhappy with your current job and would rather teach. You do not need to take an immediate financial risk by quitting your job. Instead, you could start teaching online only a few hours a week. The small beginning will help you gather feedback, improve your skills, and gain confidence.

While research is important, it is crucial to not get stuck in the research phase. Ultimately, there are no guarantees in life. You might spend substantial time on research before putting your heart into your venture and still not succeed to the degree that you want. If that happens, it is important to keep moving because *learning to be uncomfortable is also part of growth.*

There is simply no way to shortcut the time to harvest. It takes years (and decades if you dare to dream big) to see results, and the greater your vision, the greater the sacrifice—but it is all worth it.

To give an example, as Children of Infinity grew and needed more of my time, I chose to take a demotion at work so I could work fewer hours at a lower salary. I let go of the management position I had earned after years of effort. While there was a substantial financial cost, the reduced responsibilities afforded me time to invest in improving my leadership skills and reaching more people. It was one of the best decisions I have made.

EXERCISE
Taking Risks

1. What are the risks you need to take to grow in your key roles?

2. How can you mitigate the risks by starting small?

MARY'S JOURNEY

When life seems darkest, inner purpose can act as the foundation on which to build your spiritual self. Mary shares how her charmed life turned tragic and how she navigated her way down a dark path to find her soul purpose. She also illustrates the power that divine feminine energy can have in building our children's future.

The pivotal day of my spiritual transformation occurred in 1985, when I died. I had just been released from a rehabilitation center after attempting to treat my family's generational curse: addiction. Rehab, although a respite from my crumbling life, did little to help with the underlying issues that plagued me. In the two weeks that followed, while on the precipice of my death, I lost my children, my dog, and my home in a divorce that tore down the Irish Catholic life I had built.

As an obedient Catholic woman, I don't recall ever explicitly agreeing to have five children, but I certainly remember telling my husband when I was ready to stop. After a harrowing fourth pregnancy, culminating in the passing of my precious baby, I knew I couldn't go through that again.

Devastated, I, along with my doctors, pleaded that I do not become pregnant again, but my husband, who had left the seminary to marry me, opposed birth control. With little choice in the matter, I soon became pregnant with our fifth child. After another dangerous pregnancy, my son was born prematurely and barely survived. The trauma ended the marriage that had started as a fairytale.

My husband was a successful lawyer, and his wealthy family was crazy about me. I still remember the lavish wedding I'd had all those years ago and the early days of my marriage when I had lived a charmed life. Yet, I found myself alone, unable to reconcile a faith and marriage that required me to risk my life rather than use birth control. Little did I know, in the days to come, the Divine would intervene in my life and start me on the path to a spiritual transformation.

My husband made sure I lost everything in the ensuing divorce. As I sat alone in the home I was about to be ripped from, I'd had enough. I tried to end it all by "death drinking." But my death was prevented by a call from my sister, whose intuition had guided her to act as my Dickensian Ghost of Christmas Yet to Come. She revealed to me that our mother had died of alcoholism, and I was following her. Immediately, I put down my glass and got myself to the hospital, where my heart stopped.

When I died, I crossed into the angelic realm, where I was surrounded by the light of indescribable love and joy. My guides told me that my time on earth was not over yet. I was to return to the planet a changed woman tasked with bringing a new curriculum for children. I was to work globally, guiding others in this universal transformation.

Thus guided, I returned to my body in the darkest moment of my life. I was faced with the reality of having lost my children, home, and financial security. But, within days, I met my second husband, who became my rock. I was guided to move to Marshall, Minnesota, a small farm town of sixteen thousand people, and tasked with creating a learning center for children there. I didn't have a degree, or training, or a real plan to speak of, but I had divine assistance. As I connected with the community, I eventually gathered twenty-eight non-profit organizations into one room, and together we created a shared vision for the town's children. We built a community center free from government funding or interference. As anyone familiar with the bureaucracy plaguing non-profit organizations can attest, this was in and of itself a miracle.

Over the next twenty years, while working globally alongside my partners to open five new learning centers, I became the Mary of the New World. On the journey, I often felt sad that I was alienated from my children and from other family members, who thought I was crazy. But I trudged on, step by step, doing the next right thing in fulfilling my soul purpose with an innate trust that I was on the right path. My children eventually found their way back to me, including my son (whose survival after a risky pregnancy, premature birth, and tragic accident can only be described as miraculous) and my daughter, who wanted nothing to do with me but has become my protégé and trusted confidant. Now, at 86, I am not only the mother of four children but also the proud matriarch of sixteen grandchildren and three great-grandchildren as I humbly begin the next leg of this spiritual transformation.

In the summer of 2023, my soul sister introduced me to Children of Infinity. I embarked on an eight-week transformation program, and through clarity, meditation, and opening the channel to divine feminine energy, I finally have the structure and blueprint I lacked before. I strive not for perfection in this endeavor; rather, I act in good faith and trust that what must be revealed shall be. While many around my age are slowing down, I am finding new avenues to connect with millennials and guide them on the spiritual path.

I strive to be a woman of surrender, walking the path and doing what I have been called to do. I am done suffering. I am done with the crucifixion, and, instead, I live in the resurrection of the divine light. As I continue my spiritual education through daily meditation and receiving joy, wisdom, and clarity through channeling the Divine, I am honored to play a part in the symphony of planetary transformation.

Mary Regnier is a community builder and author from Minnesota.

Step 8: Honor Your Time, Attention, and Money

"Mind the moments, and the years will take care of themselves."
—Maria Edgeworth

"The toxic myth is that more is better. More of anything is better than what we have. It's the logical response if you fear there's not enough, but 'more is better' drives a competitive culture of accumulation, acquisition, and greed that only heightens fears and quickens the pace of the race."
—Lynne Twist

Creating your highest life requires wisely investing your resources: time, attention, and money.

- Time is a finite resource, and devoting time to spiritual growth requires eliminating low-value activities (such as watching TV).

- Money is a form of energy, which can be either harnessed for growth or spent on mindless consumption.

- Attention is the gateway to awareness; it can either be used to focus on what truly matters, or it can be frittered away by the next cheap stimulation.

Lacking mindful management of resources, we become lost in the endless distractions and busyness of modern life. Research shows, for example, that the average person spends about 35 hours per week watching television. That's almost a full-time job! If those hours could be invested in growth and creating value, the world would become joyous and vibrant.

The Four Ways to Spend Resources

Let's examine the four ways we can use our resources, represented by four quadrants. The quadrant structure was popularized by Stephen Covey in his book *The Seven Habits of Highly Effective People*. The key idea is that each activity you pursue belongs to one of these quadrants.

Growth	Rejuvenation
Sustenance	Waste

1. Growth

By using resources for growth, you can improve the core aspects of life—health, intelligence, relationships, finances, spirituality, and contribution. Growth is an investment because it multiplies resources. Here are some examples of good investments for personal growth:

- a time management seminar to help you use your time better
- a book on personal finances to help you live a life without financial worries
- concentration exercises to improve the quality of your attention

2. Rejuvenation

Sustained, long-term performance is impossible without adequate rest and rejuvenation. The basics are sufficient and quality sleep, relaxation, and hobbies that bring joy. In addition, periodic renewal can be achieved by creating downtime, spending time with family and friends, and activities that promote deep relaxation. Rejuvenation is as important as growth, without which we risk poor performance, stress, and burnout.

3. Sustenance

Living requires taking care of the necessities of life—paying bills, doing chores, and taking care of your car. While devoting resources to sustenance may not be exciting, the investment is necessary to keep your life running smoothly.

4. Waste

This quadrant contains unproductive (or even harmful) expenditures of resources—social media, gossip, or upgrading our gadgets even though the ones we own fulfill our needs.

Every moment and dollar we waste takes away from growth. Many people waste compulsively because they suffer from the "any-benefit mindset." This is an idea popularized by writer and professor Cal Newport in his book *Deep Work*. For example, if you ask people why they use social media, they usually offer a vague value proposition such as, "It helps me stay in touch with friends." Granted that staying in touch is a benefit, but just because something offers *some benefit* does not mean its use is justified.

You must consider the benefits not by themselves, but *in relation to the cost*. Does the investment of time justify the returns?

If you are dedicated to living your highest life, you need to get rid of the any-benefit mindset and, instead, critically examine value. Since our resources are finite, we must filter out low-value activities and pursue only the highest value ones. Just as a master craftsperson would only choose those tools that are best suited for the job at hand, you, as the crafter of your life, must choose the best tools to create joy and abundance.

How to Manage Resources Using the Quadrants

Ideally, most resources should be devoted to growth, the remaining to sustenance and rejuvenation, and none to waste. In this age of distractions and information overload, achieving this ideal is difficult but not impossible.

The key is to limit waste because it tends to eat into other quadrants. You may open Facebook to wish a friend happy birthday, only to get lost in the metaverse because Facebook's clever algorithm gets you. To prevent this, you could set a limit of 30 minutes of media consumption a day and enforce it with tools. I use software called *Freedom* that disables everything other than preselected websites. You can similarly allocate a maximum monthly budget for miscellaneous expenses. Anything that does not fit the budget can be carried over to the next month.

To optimize the sustenance quadrant, you can automate your mortgage, bills, and other financial transactions so they don't need monthly management. By growing and becoming more valuable in your profession, you can also increase your hourly rate, which will allow you to hire help to take care of household chores. For example, if you make $50 an hour, hiring help at $20 an hour is a sound financial decision.

EXERCISE
Examine Your Waste Allocation

Examine your waste quadrant and write down your answers to the following questions:

- How can you minimize the waste quadrant and move its resources to growth or rejuvenation?

- What are reasonable limits on your waste quadrant in the areas of time and money? (For example, 30 minutes a day on media, and $500 on discretionary spending a month.)

How to Honor Your Attention

The key to honoring attention is awareness. When you are aware, you can choose what seems difficult in the moment but will benefit you in the long term. For example, you might feel too tired for an evening bike ride and be tempted to watch TV instead. Yet, if you're aware of the mental resistance, you can redirect your attention to past experiences: remembering how movement revitalized you, how the fresh air elevated your mood, and how uplifted you felt by choosing action over inertia.

Awareness bridges the gap between impulse and intention, turning fleeting attention into deliberate focus.

A key aspect of attention is *concentration*—the ability to focus on a task and invest the mental energy needed to finish it. It is a skill that can be developed with practice. The longer you allow yourself to stay on task, the easier it becomes to concentrate for long periods of time and engage in what Newport calls *deep work*. Excellence in any field requires long periods of intense mental work. Think of writers, researchers, and computer programmers who write complex software that powers modern technology. Or consider a painter or sculptor dancing with their creation in a state of intense focus and experimentation.

The opposite of deep work is *shallow work.* This work is not cognitively demanding and includes low-value, administrative tasks, such as reading emails, attending meetings, and engaging with social media.

According to Dr. Newport, here is how you can develop the habit of deep work:

- Schedule large slots of time on your calendar for deep work. If you are a beginner, start with one hour of daily deep work.

- Block access to distractions, such as cell phone notifications, email, the internet, and social media.

- Focus on one task at a time.

- Give your mind periodic breaks to rest and recharge. You can set a timer to work for 45 minutes and then take a 15-minute break. During the break, unplug by taking a walk, meditating, or stretching. Do not engage in shallow work during the break.

- Track your performance daily. Write down the number of hours you have worked in a journal as a visual reminder of your performance.

- Gradually increase your deep work time to your maximum capacity, which for many people is three to four hours a day.

As you build your capacity for deep work, reflect regularly on how you can improve. Here are some guiding questions:

- What are the highest-value activities you need to focus on?

- What activities or commitments do you need to eliminate to accommodate your highest-value activities?

- What are the common distractions you face while doing important work? How can you remove them?

How to Honor Your Time

Time is our one indispensable resource. Every other resource can be replenished with the blessings of time. Lost money can be made again, health can be regained with adequate care, and even relationships can be rebuilt—but every moment we spend is irretrievably lost into the abyss of the past. Time, therefore, has to be fiercely guarded against potential thieves, such as mindless activities and the endless pursuit of consumerism.

Since there are not enough hours in a day to do everything, you must manage your priorities. *First things must come first.* Transformative work, creating a masterpiece, or becoming an exceptional leader requires doing what lies outside your comfort zone and expending mental energy. Furthermore, you will need to maintain the focus for years, even decades. Here are five steps to managing your priorities well:

1. **Clarify outcomes.** List your key focus areas and write down your ideal outcomes for each. The outcomes can fall into one or more of the following three categories: products, learning, and practice.

- *Products* are tangible or intangible creations, such as a book you want to write.

- *Learning* helps you to develop specific skills. You will need to master writing in order to draft a book.

- *Practice* relates to consistently doing activities that produce results. Writing 500 words a day is a crucial practice for drafting a book.

As an example, here are my four key focus areas, followed by a table of my ideal outcomes:

- **Communication.** Create content (for example, books, lectures, and video lessons), informal communication (such as emails), and activities needed for Children of Infinity's growth (such as marketing).

- **Productivity.** Manage my time well and produce every day.

- **Spiritual Growth.** Do my spiritual practices daily to maintain a high vibration and receive guidance from my Higher Self.

- **Leadership.** Help members of the community progress. New community members need guidance to become practitioners. Practitioners need guidance to become volunteers and leaders. In addition, I lead people belonging to other organizations.

Focus Area	Product	Learning	Practice
Communication	Create one video lesson every week. Write books.	Become a better writer.	Write Read
Spiritual Growth			Meditate
Leadership		Read/listen to resources on leadership.	Read Listen Guide others.
Health			Exercise daily.

2. **Define the regimen.** Achieving an outcome requires doing specific activities consistently for a set amount of time. Here are the steps:

   a. Write down the daily and weekly activities needed to achieve the outcome.
   b. Determine how much time to devote to each activity. (For cognitively demanding tasks, an uninterrupted stretch of 30 to 45 minutes is a good start.)
   c. Allocate time for each activity.

Continuing from the table above, here are my activities based on their outcomes.

Focus Area	Product	Learning	Practice	Activity
Communication	Create two video lessons every week. Write this book.	Become a better writer.	Write Read	Write for 2 hours. Read for 30 minutes.
Spiritual Growth			Meditate	Meditate for 60 minutes.
Leadership		Read/listen to resources on leadership.	Read Listen	Read or listen for 30 minutes.
Health			Exercise daily.	Exercise for 45 minutes a day.

3. **Create a stack of priorities.** Take all of your activities and prioritize them in one stack. For example, here is my list:

   a. Meditate: 60 minutes
   b. Write: 45 minutes
   c. Exercise: 15 minutes
   d. Write: 45 minutes
   e. Exercise: 15 minutes

f. Write: 30 minutes

g. Read about writing: 30 minutes

h. Read/listen to material on leadership: 30 minutes

4. **Schedule the activities.** Write a simple checklist and note the time actually spent on each task. Remember, *you cannot improve what you do not measure.* Schedule your most important tasks in the morning because finishing them creates a feeling of accomplishment and builds momentum; it then becomes easier to maintain momentum and keep succeeding.

Here is the schedule I follow:

Task	Time Slot	Done	Time Spent
Meditate for 60 minutes.	5:15 - 6:15 a.m.		
Write for 45 minutes.	6:30 - 7:15 a.m.		
Exercise for 15 minutes.	7:15 - 7:30 a.m.		
Write for 45 minutes.	7:30 - 8:15 a.m.		
Exercise for 15 minutes.	8:15 - 8:30 a.m.		
Write for 30 minutes.	8:30 - 9:00 a.m.		
Read about writing for 30 minutes.	9:00 - 9:30 a.m.		
Read/listen to material on leadership for 30 minutes.	Listen while waiting, doing chores, or driving.		

5. **Do a weekly review.** Here are a few things to include in the review:

- *Review and adjust.* Review your focus areas, outcomes, and activities weekly, and ensure they remain consistent with your priorities. Your priorities may change, or you may find better ways to accomplish results. Adjust accordingly.

- *Assess your effectiveness.* Are you achieving your goals every week? If not, what is blocking you? What can you do better? What changes could make you more productive?

- *Experiment.* Follow the schedule for a week and change next week's schedule based on the reflection from this week. This allows the balance between structure (which comes from following a hard list of stacked priorities) and flexibility.

How to Honor Your Money

Our relationship with money is complicated because of value judgments such as, "money is the root of all evil," or "money solves all problems." These judgments elevate money from a mere means of exchange to a source of emotions. Many attach such high value to money that their entire self-worth depends on their bank account.

A healthy relationship with money starts with understanding what money is and how it helps you live your highest life. From a spiritual perspective, money is energy. The best use of this energy is to support your life's purpose. True abundance is the ability to live your purpose with ease, and money is a helpful tool.

In a capitalistic society, money is the primary tool for exchange of value. Just like any other tool, working with a broken or inadequate tool for exchanging value will prevent you from achieving your objective, which is to live your highest life.

The foundation of financial success is your attitude toward money. The wrong attitude puts people in one of two unhealthy categories:

1. **Money slaves.** For these people, money becomes a god, and its pursuit the primary purpose of their lives. Whether or not they express their infatuation with money outwardly, they spend

most of their time and energy earning and spending money, not realizing that their lives have become fodder for the endless cycle of consumption. An expensive lifestyle—a common hallmark of money slaves—becomes a *golden cage* because working is required to sustain the lifestyle. This is a no-win situation because the pursuit of a better lifestyle never ends.

2. Money repellers. People in this category believe that money is somehow evil. This limiting belief prevents them from learning about money and leads to financial struggles that hinder fulfilling their life purpose. This limiting belief, emphasized heavily in some spiritual traditions, instills in adherents a false piety: they consider themselves "above" money. This piety often masks intellectual laziness and feelings of inadequacy about money. Incompetence with money forces people to live a suboptimal life involving constant financial struggle and stress.

Money is a tool—*nothing more, nothing less*. A tool is valuable, not by itself, but because it helps you to achieve your life's purpose. It is important to learn how to create financial stability and abundance to live your highest life.

EXERCISE
Examine Your Relationship with Money

Write down your answers to the following questions:

- On your life path, what has your relationship with money been like?
- How can you cultivate a more conscious and empowering relationship with money?
- What steps should you take to use money as a tool rather than a goal?

The Relationship Between Money and Happiness

To create a healthy relationship with money, it is vital to understand the relationship between money and happiness. Money does increase your level of happiness and well-being; however, the increase is not uniform. The chart below, based on research by Nobel Prize-winning economist Daniel Kahneman, shows the approximate relationship between money and happiness. As we make more money, our overall level of happiness increases, but then it reaches a point where additional money does not make us happier.

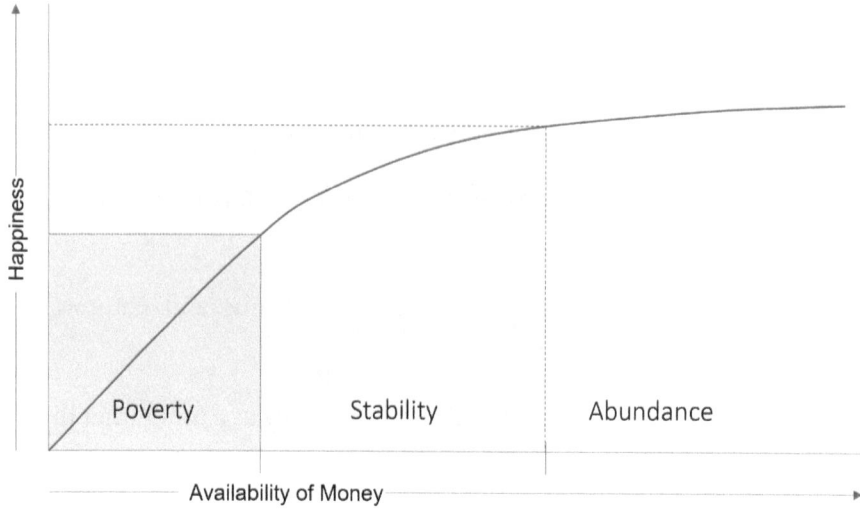

The relationship between money and happiness has three phases:

1. **Phase I—Poverty:** When people lack sufficient money to take care of basic needs, money brings direct happiness because basic needs largely determine our happiness. In this phase, it's important to learn about earning and managing money so you can escape poverty as quickly as possible.

2. **Phase II—Stability:** In this phase, one's basic needs are met, and some money is available for discretionary spending. The relationship between money and happiness is no longer linear. The curve begins to flatten; thus, additional money does not make you as happy as it did in the poverty phase. During the stability phase, it's important to use discretionary financial resources to learn more about money, to develop your skills, and to align your life with purpose, rather than being controlled by the consumerist agenda.

3. **Phase III—Abundance:** In the third phase, more money brings minimal additional happiness because both basic and discretionary

needs are met. Daniel Kahneman's research shows that, ultimately, there is an income level at which money can buy things but does not make you happier. When the study was published in 2010, the researchers' estimate for the threshold income was $75,000 per year for people living in the United States. With inflation, this level has likely increased to the $100,000-$150,000 range, and, of course, it depends on the cost of living in your area. The important mental leap in this phase is to free yourself from the *compulsion* to keep making money, since such a compulsion will prevent you from devoting yourself to living your life's purpose. Focus on what makes you come alive rather than earning an even richer living.

The Three Pillars of Financial Abundance

If you want to be financially abundant, there are three key areas you need to master: saving, earning, and investing. Let's dive into each.

SAVING

"If you cannot save money, the seeds of greatness are not in you."

—W. Clement Stone

I consider saving the most important pillar of financial success, even more important than earning. If you do not save, you will spend all you earn and then some. With *credit,* you can spend before you earn and get into debt. This eats into your earnings because you must pay interest, which requires you to earn more just to break even. More importantly, debt also creates a heavy psychological burden.

A cautionary example of reckless spending is Johnny Depp, the famous movie star. It is estimated that between 2003 and 2016, he earned over $650 million from movies and endorsements. He spent it all on a lavish lifestyle and eventually got into a messy public lawsuit with TMG, his management firm. TMG revealed that Depp squandered his fortune on expensive items, such as a yacht that cost $8 million to buy, $10 million to restore, and $350,000 a month to maintain. As astounding as Depp's story is, he is hardly an outlier. Most people can't resist the tempting ads that tell us we deserve things that, in truth, we don't need. We become victims of worthless distractions that cost a fortune.

A spiritually enlightened way of living values peace of mind, which requires sound financial management. By consciously *conserving* money, you can get the maximum value from it. Here are four rules for saving money:

>   1. **Spend only what you have.** Stop buying what you don't have the money to pay for. The easiest way to do this is to freeze your credit cards and use a debit card to pay for all purchases. If you must use credit cards to build credit, set up an automatic payment to pay the entire balance each month. If you are in debt, be honest about your financial situation. Being honest with yourself will prevent you from spending when you cannot afford to.
>
>   2. **Save before you spend.** Parkinson's law for money states, "Expenses expand to fill income." If you don't save intentionally, you will, by default, spend all you earn. To break this vicious cycle, make a portion of your income unavailable for spending. Use an automated savings program that allocates a portion of your paycheck to savings.
>
>   3. **Look at each expense critically.** The maze of consumerism is full of shiny objects designed to make you forget the core utility of money: to live your life purpose. To avoid this maze, critically examine every expense. Is the proposed expense a need or a want? Which of the four quadrants does the expenditure belong to? Does

it help you live your life's purpose? *The best purchases are those you never make.*

4. **Live frugally.** According to the book *The Millionaire Next Door*, frugality is the first trait of first-generation millionaires. Get high value for your money by demanding more from every dollar. Instead of buying new things, consider buying used or refurbished items. When choosing between two items, instead of asking which one is *better*, ask yourself, *which one is sufficient to fulfill my needs?*

EXERCISE
Implement a Basic Saving Routine

1. Choose a percentage of your income to save monthly (I recommend saving at least 15%).

2. Set up your bank to deduct this amount automatically every month and transfer it to a savings account.

EARNING

The recipe for earning more money is simple: acquire skills that make you more valuable. We are extremely fortunate to live in a knowledge economy in which we can create wealth by acquiring and applying knowledge rather than from capital or manpower. Some of the biggest companies in the world, such as Google, deal primarily with information rather than industrial equipment or manufacturing.

The flip side of information, however, is that as information increases, it becomes harder to differentiate the signal from the noise—that is, to determine what is worth paying attention to. Further, the ability to distill knowledge from information presents a great opportunity.

Here are the critical skills that make you valuable in today's marketplace:

1. **Learn difficult things.** Our rapidly changing world needs and rewards people who can quickly master complex systems. For example, the field of software pays high salaries because software programming is constantly evolving with new languages, new internet paradigms, and smart technology. But you don't need to be in a fancy industry to profit from the basic principle: Identify skills that are valued in your industry and master them. You can attend training programs, read books and articles, take online courses, and get certifications to improve your skills. Stay up to date with the latest trends and technologies in your industry. Many employers also pay tuition to help you develop your skills.

2. **Produce quality work.** When you produce work that exceeds expectations and can do so unsupervised, you free up your employer's precious resources to focus on other priorities. The better the quality of your work, the more the market will compensate you, so resolve to *go the extra mile*. By focusing on achieving results and consistently exceeding expectations, you become more valuable to your industry and unlock the opportunities to earn more.

3. **Take responsibility.** Employees who take responsibility are rare; thus, they are highly rewarded. Become the person your organization can count on when needed. Don't merely do the work, *own your work* by taking the initiative to improve the underlying processes and workflows. Try innovative approaches to solve the problems your organization faces. When you act like an owner rather than an employee, you unlock the highest potential for professional success.

4. Lead. Your real earning potential is unlocked at leadership levels. Seek opportunities to take on more responsibilities in your job. Don't wait for your boss to assign tasks to you—take initiative and identify areas where you can contribute more, then see the projects through to completion.

5. Invest in your communication skills. Communication is a vital aspect of any job, but it is even more important in the knowledge economy, where ideas can be extremely valuable. Work on improving your written and verbal communication skills. Good communication skills will help you to increase your influence and help your organization achieve its objectives.

EXERCISE
Professional Skills Assessment and Plan

1. What skills will make you more valuable professionally? If you have a job, seek feedback from your employer.
2. Create a plan to acquire the professional skills you need.

INVEST

You can grow your money by investing it. By having a disciplined approach to investing, you can eventually achieve financial independence—a stage where the returns from your investments are sufficient to cover your expenses. For example, if you own a rental property, you could live off the monthly rent you get from the tenants.

There are many ways to invest. Based on your temperament and inclination, one of them will be better for you than the others. Here are the four common vehicles to financial independence:

1. **Real estate.** Real estate investing offers tax advantages, leverage (the ability to borrow from banks), and cashflow (monthly rental income)—all with a manageable time commitment, which was key for me when I started my investing journey while still having a full-time job. In 2011, when the property market had tanked after the 2008 financial crisis, I bought a condo on a short sale (which means it was for sale at less than the mortgage owed on it). When the market bounced back in 2016, I sold it at a profit. The best part was that the gain was tax-free since it was our primary residence. I used the gain to purchase a rental building. I fixed up the building and have rented it out over the ensuing years, creating a modest cash flow.

    Caution: Despite the marketing hype surrounding real estate investing, I have found it is neither easy nor quick. If real estate interests you, I recommend starting with a small property to learn the basics, then expanding to bigger properties as your portfolio grows.

2. **Your own business.** Small business is at the heart of the American enterprise. If you have business acumen, you can find a way to deliver value to the market and innovate along the way. You don't even need to have a business idea of your own; you can buy an existing business (a franchise, for example) with a proven success system you can replicate.

The goal is to create a business that can operate and generate profits *without* needing much direct involvement. Thus, owning a business is not just about being self-employed but about creating true leverage.

3. **Intellectual property.** If you are willing to invest the time to gain expertise in a field, you can create intellectual property in the form of books, courses, seminars, and so forth, which can generate passive income. With the explosion of online learning, there is a huge opportunity to tap into global markets. Attractively, intellectual property does not require the huge financial investment one needs for real property. The journey to expertise is not easy, however, and making a substantial income from intellectual property involves the crucial step of marketing. But if you are passionate about learning and communicating, this could be a fruitful financial vehicle for you.

4. **Paper assets.** Stocks, bonds, and other financial instruments may offer a path to grow your money, but this path is tricky. The barrier to entry is low (you can call yourself an investor at the click of a button). Compared to real estate, which requires months of due diligence and bank approvals, owning paper assets is child's play. The downside is that paper assets do not offer the benefits of leverage, tax-free gains, and cash flow. Having seen the 2008 financial crisis, cryptocurrency crashes, and various other cycles in the stock market, I would advise caution if you choose to invest in paper assets. Dedicate sufficient time to learn more before investing money in paper assets. I personally don't invest in them.

Gaining financial abundance requires a willingness to educate yourself about money, a systematic approach to investing, and above all, discipline. In most cases, it takes decades to reach financial abundance and, eventually, financial independence. If you find the length of this road discouraging, please remember that *money is a tool, not a goal.*

On the spiritual journey, money is fundamentally an energy to be mastered. As lightworkers, it is our responsibility to use this energy to bring love and light to the planet. For example, Children of Infinity, the non-profit I created, needed around $35,000 in the first three years to build an online platform, create videos, advertise, and buy tools such as Zoom subscriptions. Fortunately, I'd managed my money well and had savings available to donate. This contribution has already helped thousands of people learn about spiritual principles and how to be part of a conscious community. By managing your money well, you too can use it to bring light to others.

SARA'S JOURNEY

Our interpersonal relationships are shaped by our level of consciousness. As we become more aware of our relationship patterns, they can become a catalyst for spiritual transformation. Sara shares how she grew through difficult romantic relationships and tragic circumstances to find her spiritual path.

I have been fortunate to experience contentment in the physical aspects of life. Growing up, our family of nine was far from rich, yet we thrived on the simplicity of a minimalist lifestyle. After being conceived in Cambodia in 1967, where my parents were part of the Subud spiritual movement, my family returned to the US, where, during my upbringing, I was immersed in spirituality and meditation. My parents were perpetual seekers. I can recall my father spending hours in meditation and study as he and my mother forged their own spiritual path. Though steadfast in their spiritual endeavors, my parents never pushed me to conform to any specific belief system. They encouraged me to discover my own path.

My relationships with my learned yet troubled father and sweet but terribly anxious mother became my first model of codependency. I became one of the "walking wounded," just like my parents. Luckily, the string of challenging interpersonal relationships to follow would come with a purpose, placing me on a path to spiritual transformation and enabling me to evolve in the pursuit of my soul's purpose.

Upon turning 18, I left the spiritual and physical refuge of my family and childhood home to pursue higher education. In the early 2000s, after earning an associate degree, I became a stay-at-home mom and wife to my first husband before ultimately returning to acquire a bachelor's degree in health information technology. Our marriage turned tumultuous as it became clear that my new husband used alcohol addiction to deal with his childhood wounds. After a decade, the marriage ended. The divorce and subsequent shunning by my in-laws would become the catalyst for my first spiritual awakening, which occurred as I rebuilt myself from scratch. At this time, I focused heavily on psychological development and personal growth. Poised, and with newfound strength, I remarried. But I was once again blindsided by my new partner's unhealed wounds from childhood abuse. Once his wounds and subsequent harmful behaviors became apparent, I realized his demons were too powerful for me to slay, and we had a friendly divorce. I even allowed him continued access to my children, hoping that forgiveness, love, and family would help him heal. Unfortunately, his wounds were too deep, and a few years after our separation, he killed himself.

The trauma of finding his dead body as I walked into his house demanded a lifetime of healing on its own, but that turned out to be just the beginning. Following my ex-husband's death, my romantic partner at the time ghosted me, and a close friend passed away only three weeks later. This series of grief-trauma shattered my psyche in a way that demanded it be rebuilt entirely. I dedicated myself to the reconstruction of my Self, this time focusing on my spiritual foundation. I shed worldly responsibilities to make room for a spiritual awakening. As I gained insight into my spiritual being, I realized that I had been unconsciously attracting deeply wounded men. Upon taking responsibility for the dysfunctional and codependent patterns of my relationships, I saw that these had been passed down generationally in my family. I spent the next three years focusing on deliberate healing without a romantic partner, certain that the perceived safety of being in a relationship was just an illusion; unless I reshaped my inner patterns of connecting, my relationships would continue down an unhealthy path.

In the summer of 2022, I found a gateway to spiritual growth through Children of Infinity. I participated in a yearlong program involving reading and assimilating spiritually empowering books. When I read *Power vs. Force* by David R. Hawkins, it all started to click. Robert Schwartz's *Your Soul's Gift* helped me to reconcile my second husband's suicide in a way I couldn't before. Through the Quantum Hypnosis Healing Technique (QHHT), I understood the law of karma and how it affected my attachments in relationships, not only in this life, but in past lives as well.

Though I have been a seeker all my life, I now have a supportive community to help guide me. My success in evolving and raising my consciousness has translated into my relationships. It is no accident that after healing in this way, I find myself in the first healthy relationship I've had in this life. I am with a man who is healthy, doesn't drink or smoke, and doesn't have any childhood trauma. I entered this budding relationship with open eyes and without expectation, trusting that all would be as it should.

I feel transformed by the inner work I have undertaken over the last several years. Now open to a new way of relating to the world, I am drawn to using the gift of my voice. I am yet to determine if I am called to use this gift through singing, guided meditation, or counseling, but I am excited to see where this endeavor will lead me.

I continue to meditate, read, and learn—happily hopping down the rabbit holes to get to the spiritual mysteries underneath. I am determined to use my time on Earth to be the light for lost people and offer them healing.

Sara (name changed) wishes to remain anonymous.

Step 9: Transform Your Health

"The greatest of follies is to sacrifice health for any other kind of happiness."
—Arthur Schopenhauer

"Health gives hope, and hope gives everything else."
—Thomas Carlyle

The human body is a biological marvel of incredible complexity: despite significant progress made in life sciences, we still have much to learn about its remarkable anatomical systems.

From a spiritual perspective, the body is an instrument through which consciousness experiences physical reality. Maintaining a healthy body helps one to learn, grow, create, serve, and attain higher states of consciousness. Conversely, when the body is neglected, it can become an impediment to spiritual growth.

To maintain a healthy body so you can more easily fulfill your soul purpose, focus on the three keys to physical well-being: nutrition, movement, and rest.

Nutrition

What we consume affects not only our physical health but also our emotional and spiritual well-being. While the spiritual aspect of food is often overlooked in Western culture, it is highly valued in the yogic system. The yogic worldview emphasizes that food affects not only our physical body but also the energy body, which informs our consciousness.

Selecting spiritually nourishing **food** that enhances our overall well-being, as well as consuming enough **water** and being out in **nature**, are vitally important. The following sections explore these three components of nutrition.

Food

We are fortunate to have over 50 years of research on food's long-term effects. Dr. T. Colin Campbell, a professor of nutritional biochemistry at Cornell University, spearheaded the China Study. This research project, which began in 1983 and was conducted by Cornell University, the University of Oxford, and the Chinese Academy of Preventive Medicine, investigated the correlation between nutrition and rates of cancer, heart disease, and metabolic disorders. Dr. Campbell has written extensively on the study's findings in his books *The China Study* (2005) and *Whole* (2014). Here are the key points from his research:

- The optimal food for the human body is plant-based food in forms as close to their natural state as possible ("whole foods"). Eat a variety of vegetables, fruits, raw nuts and seeds, beans and legumes, and whole grains. Avoid heavily processed foods and animal products, as well as added salt, oil, and sugar. Aim to get 80 percent of your calories from carbohydrates, 10 percent from fat, and 10 percent from protein.

- What you eat every day matters more to your health than your DNA or most of the toxic chemicals lurking in your environment.

- Food can heal you faster and more profoundly than drugs.

- Healthy food choices can prevent most of the dangerous diseases we face, including cancer, heart disease, Type 2 diabetes, stroke, macular degeneration, migraines, and arthritis.

Subsequent research across a range of countries and populations has verified a correlation between the consumption of meat and an increased risk of cancer. The correlation is particularly strong with red and processed meat.

In 2015, the International Agency for Research on Cancer (IARC), which is part of the World Health Organization (WHO), published a report concluding that "processed meat was classified as carcinogenic to humans (Group 1), based on sufficient evidence in humans that the consumption of processed meat causes colorectal cancer."

While the exact mechanisms behind this association are not yet fully understood, it is believed that certain compounds in meat—including heterocyclic amines, polycyclic aromatic hydrocarbons, and heme iron—are highly toxic. Blood testing done after the consumption of even just one meat-based meal has shown inflammation in the human body, indicating that it essentially rejects meat and attempts to protect itself. Subjecting the body to the inflammation caused by meat consumption on a regular basis leads to toxicity and severe health conditions such as heart disease, obesity, and high blood pressure.

One theory as to why the human body is incompatible with meat consumption is that our intestines are much longer than those of carnivores. Compared to plants, meat rots quickly and must be eliminated from the system as soon as possible, which is where intestine length comes into play. The length of carnivore intestines is much shorter (3-6 times the body length) compared to humans (10-12 times). When a carnivore eats meat, therefore, the meat is quickly eliminated from the animal's system. Whereas when humans eat meat, it stays in our systems for much longer and produces toxins.

What about research promoting meat?

Despite the WHO warning, meat consumption has increased from 2015 to 2023, the reason being that these findings have not reached the average meat consumer—to the contrary, most meat eaters still think meat is an essential source of protein and is healthy.

The main problem is the powerful meat lobby, which manufactures its own "research" that tries to play down the risks of meat. The meat industry, like many others, chases profits. This leads to bias in studies conducted by researchers with ties to the industry. A 2019 study published by a research team headed by Bradley C. Johnston, for instance, concluded that eating red meat has no effect on health. An investigation by the *Washington Post* found, however, that the study had not disclosed Johnston's connection to the Agriculture and Life Sciences (AgriLife) program at Texas A&M, which is partly funded by the beef industry. Furthermore, it is noteworthy that Johnston did not disclose a conflict of interest in a similar study published by the Annals of Internal Medicine (2016) aimed at debunking sugar consumption's association with health risks. That study was funded by the International Life Sciences Institute, which has been supported by McDonald's, Coca-Cola, PepsiCo, and Cargill.

This misinformation campaign by the meat industry (and there are similar campaigns by other sectors of the food industry) requires you to carefully examine the source of funding for health research. If you want objective research, I recommend watching the documentary *The Game Changers*, which explores the benefits of a plant-based diet. The film features several elite athletes who adopted a plant-based diet and achieved remarkable success. An example is Scott Jurek, an ultramarathoner who can run for days on minimal sleep. The film also presents scientific evidence showing that a plant-based diet improves health, reduces the risk of chronic diseases, and increases athletic performance. The documentary challenges common misconceptions about meat and protein, and it encourages viewers to consider the impact of their food choices on their health and the environment.

The Effects of Food Production on Ecology

Another reason to avoid meat is that commercial meat production is the leading cause of ecological degradation. Industrial meat production consumes large amounts of resources, such as water, grain, and topsoil. Producing one pound of feedlot beef, for example, takes 2500 gallons of water, 12 pounds of grain, 35 pounds of topsoil, and the energy equivalent of 1 gallon of gasoline. Cattle farming for meat has become a significant ecological problem, as 70% of US grain production is fed to livestock, resulting in the destruction of forests. Additionally, animal agriculture is a major contributor to water pollution and produces ten times more waste than the human population.

Spirituality and the Consumption of Meat

From a spiritual perspective, it's cruel to slaughter animals and eat them while there are alternatives available. The spiritual ideal is to *lessen the suffering of all sentient beings,* which includes animals.

Food is not merely for the body; it also has a spiritual essence, called *prana,* which informs spiritual growth. Meat carries the lowest form of prana (tamasic) and creates animalistic tendencies in its consumers:

cruelty, excessive attachment to pleasure, and a materially focused life that neglects the spiritual dimension. That is why yogic traditions prohibit meat consumption for spiritual seekers.

As discussed in Step 6, the more evolved the animal, the more toxic its meat is for humans. You can stop consuming meat in phases and move toward a more compassionate and spiritually aligned way of life.

The Danger of Processed Foods

While it's crucial to remove meat and other animal products from your diet, removing those alone is not enough for optimal health—you must also avoid consuming processed foods.

Commercial food processing prioritizes profit over well-being and our planet's health. The quest for profit values not nutrition, but volume and shelf life, which are achieved by using additives such as salt, sugar, fat, and chemicals, which make food toxic. Furthermore, in a market economy, companies do not wait for research on the consequences of their practices. Their narrow-sighted focus is to reap profits today without considering the long-term harm they cause. It's no wonder that unhealthy foods, such as potato chips, canned goods, and soda, have become staples in our diets. As conscious beings, we must be mindful of the businesses we support with our choices.

In addition to being a source of nutrition, food is a source of spiritual energy. If you are committed to spiritual growth, it is crucial to be mindful of the intention that goes into preparing your food. Commercially prepared food, motivated by profit, may lower your vibration due to the selfish energy it carries.

Instead of entrusting your health to others, cooking at home gives you control over what you put in your body. Cooking and eating with family have been important rituals throughout human history because they create bonding and help pass culinary knowledge from generation to generation. Unfortunately, in today's fast-paced world, people consider themselves too busy to cook and thus have lost touch with this tradition. It's time to rediscover the joy of cooking and reap the rewards of good nutrition and social bonding.

Even if you are single and cook alone, food cooked at home is better because you can choose healthy ingredients. To infuse your food with a higher vibration, you can prepare meals while listening to spiritually uplifting material, music, and chants.

Water

Water, which constitutes around 60 percent of the human body, is essential for optimal functioning. In our coffee-driven culture, many people suffer from chronic dehydration without even realizing it. When they feel hungry, it is often a sign of thirst, and popular beverages, such as coffee and alcohol, further dehydrate the body because they are diuretic.

Fortunately, it's easy to access clean and refreshing water. Rather than relying on environmentally harmful bottled water, simply install an active charcoal water filter at home. These filters effectively remove toxins such as chlorine and lead from tap water, making it a healthy and sustainable option for hydration. Carry your filtered water in a reusable bottle.

Taking time to hydrate also gives you greater access to intuitive wisdom. Spiritually, water serves as a conduit for energy to move and work through your body. Sufficient hydration is crucial for healing and for channeling spiritual energy.

Nature

Connecting with nature is crucial for maintaining a healthy balance of energy. Through most of human history, this connection was as natural as breathing. With cities becoming the hubs of modern living, however, we have lost access to this connection.

Simply being in nature and connecting with the Earth allows your body's energy field to rejuvenate and rebalance. Spending at least 20 minutes each day in sunlight also stimulates vitamin D synthesis in your body, which is essential for balancing numerous bodily functions. According to research, vitamin D is not only a vitamin but also a multifunctional hormone (or prohormone) essential for overall health, including the immune system, the cardiovascular system, the endocrine system, and other metabolic pathways. There is also evidence that vitamin D deficiency can cause depression, pain, and cancer.

The Sun sustains life on the earth, and also provides spiritual energy, or prana. Take time to bask in sunlight, in nature if you can. Yogic postures, such as the sun salutation, can further enhance your prana.

Movement

The human body is meant to move. In the book *Spark: The Revolutionary New Science of Exercise and the Brain* (2008), John J. Ratey emphasizes that exercise improves not only physical health but also cognitive abilities such as learning, memory, and mood. The book provides scientific evidence to support the case that regular exercise helps to prevent and treat various neurological conditions, including depression, anxiety, ADHD, and dementia. It also emphasizes the importance of incorporating enjoyable forms of exercise into daily life and encourages readers to commit to regular physical activity for their well-being.

Many people want to exercise more, but they limit themselves by thinking of exercise as something you can only do with machines in a gym. The key to sustained physical activity, however, is that *movement should be as natural as breathing*. The best physical activity engages the mind along with the body, such as playing a sport. You can also try mindful forms of movement, such as yoga, Qi Gong, or Tai Chi. Other activities, such as dancing, hiking, jogging, walking, group training, and biking, can be excellent forms of movement.

In many spiritual traditions, rhythmic movements and dance were used to raise one's vibration and to access higher states of awareness. The practice is still used by tribes across the world. The key is to find something that feels natural and that works for you. It is worth trying different activities until you find one you love.

Rest and Relaxation

A well-rested body serves as your greatest physical, mental, and psychological asset.

Many people in our hyperactive culture incorrectly believe that rest is optional. Highly driven individuals often sacrifice sleep for work, not realizing that sleep deprivation can cause physical and cognitive problems, including fatigue, irritability, impaired judgment and reaction time, reduced immune function, and an increased risk of accidents and chronic diseases.

Our bodies cannot perform optimally without adequate rest and relaxation. The more we rest, the better we can perform. I encourage you to prioritize rest. Make it part of your routine by creating a pre-sleep ritual that you follow before going to bed. This routine starts an hour before you plan to sleep. During this time, avoid all screens, including your phone and computer. The blue light from modern LED screens has been shown to interfere with sleep. Engage in activities that help you to relax, such as reading, listening to music, and spending time with loved ones. By ensuring you get quality sleep, you will have more energy throughout the day, which you need to show up as your best self.

EXERCISE
Improve Your Health

- Watch the documentary *The Game Changers*.
- List action items to create better eating habits.
- Select one form of movement you love and incorporate it into your daily life.
- Create a routine for winding down every day.

The body is the vessel for consciousness. The better you take care of it through adequate nutrition, movement, and rest, the greater vitality you will have to pursue your boldest visions.

BRENDA'S JOURNEY

Spiritual transformation leads to self-awareness, which heals relationships. Brenda shares how, through spiritual growth, she healed her relationships with the people she loves the most.

On my spiritual journey, I have transformed from a controlling mother to a compassionate one, and my tumultuous relationship with my only son has healed. As I reflect on this journey, I realize that my need to control resulted from my own impoverished and chaotic childhood.

My life on this Earth began in suffering. Born in poverty to American Indian parents, I was the middle daughter of 12 children, of whom only nine survived. My dad, a miner with an eighth-grade education, worked long hours to provide what little we had. To make matters worse, I was born with a displaced hip and needed a corrective brace as a toddler. During this time, and again at the age of 11 when my hip was displaced a second time, I was given justifiable yet inequitable attention and protection from my parents.

I persevered amidst challenges and became one of the few in my family to graduate high school. I looked forward to attending college. However, I couldn't enroll because my father, unable to understand the bureaucracy of financial aid, refused to sign the paperwork.

My future looked bleak, but I refused to accept a life of poverty for me and my young son. I educated myself about money so I could give my child what I never had, and I discovered a path to financial success through real estate investing. With little money, I had to use a lot of creativity to buy properties, but through hard work and luck, I eventually created enough cash flow to retire.

Although I achieved financial freedom, my underlying anxiety about money and the fear of my child living a life of suffering led me to be an overprotective and controlling mother. As my son matured, he naturally resented and resisted my control. My unhealthy behavior toward him continued, I am ashamed to say, even after he married and became a father.

The quest to heal my relationship has been a spiritual one. From early childhood, I was a devout Catholic. My journey to spiritual transformation began the day I lost my faith in Catholicism. It was the late 1980s, and along with questionable fashion trends, the AIDS epidemic had made its way to my small Colorado town. As I sat in a pew beside my young son in a church that was more like a second home to me, I listened as the priest proclaimed that those dying from AIDS would burn in hell. Having lost loved ones to the disease, I was horrified at the raw hatred. Unable to tolerate it any longer, I grabbed my son's hand and walked out of the church. I knew that I had outgrown the Catholic Church's teachings and that if I wanted to experience further growth, I had to seek it elsewhere.

I attended the Unity Church nearby, as well as every other church I could find within my travel radius. Religion was the only path to spirituality that I knew, but I discovered that my spirit did not align with any of the churches. I even tried a one-size-fits-all faith but felt like a misshaped peg trying to force my way into a religious circle. And so, just shy of 30 years old, I came to the realization that I would not find the answers through religion. I still believed that Jesus was here, and that he came to teach about love, but I was done with religion.

Although I stopped searching for answers within religion, my quest for knowledge continued through personal growth. In the late '80s, I met a woman far ahead of her time who was creating a business out of self-awareness training. This woke me up to the idea that the answers to our deepest questions lie within. But putting the puzzle together took years of patient seeking. As my awareness grew, I decided to take an ancestry class to delve deeper into my Native heritage and generational trauma. During the class, I learned that connecting with higher wisdom requires contemplative practices such as meditation. Although the meditation training they offered was rudimentary, it got me started on the inner journey. I found comfort in the answers revealed through this endeavor but still struggled greatly in my relationship with my son.

Still seeking to heal my relationship with my son, I found Children of Infinity in 2023 and immediately found effective tools. Upon joining, I took advantage of a free course to learn about non-duality and the evolution of consciousness. As I continued progressing and learned about pre-birth planning, I came to realize that my lessons applied not only to my relationship with my son but also to my parents, extended family, and Native ancestry. It was clear that I had to heal all these relationships to find peace.

After studying empathetic communication with a support group within the community, I've finally learned to be less reactive and to listen without judgment when communicating with my son. I can now recognize the actions of my parents and other loved ones through the lens of compassion and empathy. There is profound healing in understanding. Once I began repairing the spiritual foundations of my relationships, I was able to move toward my soul purpose, knowing that my ancestors, along with future generations, would be the wind at my back instead of stumbling blocks along my path.

I have come to the realization that it is not my responsibility to protect my adult child or to interfere with his or anyone else's life path. Each of us comes from Source and must learn lessons according to our pre-birth plan. I have learned to honor my son's space to find and live in his truth, as I find and live in mine. Our relationship has transformed through this process of awakening and understanding. We haven't had an argument in six months, which is a miracle. Just a few days ago, my son and I shared a meal, and I just listened to him talk about his life. That was it. I realized that all he wanted was the attention, love, and support of his mother, nothing more.

As I grow in awareness, I am volunteering to channel that maternal, protective energy into guiding children in this confusing world. My wish is that every human being finds sanctuary in loving relationships.

Brenda Martinez is a community facilitator for Children of Infinity.

Step 10: Transform Your Relationships

> Not by toiling through tomes of great size,
> Does wisdom come to light our eyes,
> But love, a word so short and meek,
> Leads us to the knowing we seek.
>
> —Kabir, Indian poet-saint

On the human journey, we learn our most important lessons through relationships. It is relationships that provide the opportunity to learn about love, sharing, empathy, companionship, and joy. According to pre-birth planning, people in our life are there to honor a mutual agreement. This holds true of family, friends, and romantic and professional relationships. When aligned with higher consciousness, relationships become a source of joy; conversely, when aligned with lower consciousness, they create struggle and sorrow.

The primary determinant of our relationship experience is *our level of consciousness*. I introduced the three levels of consciousness in Step 3. Let's dive deeper into how they create the foundation for relationships.

Tamas (Powerlessness)

Powerlessness, the lowest state of consciousness, is also the most common one because humans are born into it. As babies, we come into the world helpless and dependent on caregivers for food, shelter, and protection.

Our power expands as we grow and learn to communicate through language, take care of physical needs, and develop independent thinking. Recognizing and expressing our power is the first marker of spiritual progress.

According to spiritual teacher Carolyn Myss, there are four archetypes of powerlessness: the child, the victim, the prostitute, and the saboteur. Each archetype has unique characteristics in its expression of a lack of spiritual power.

The key to working with these archetypes is to use them as tools for self-awareness and growth by understanding the limitations they represent. By recognizing the archetypes in yourself, you can become aware of the limitations you need to overcome.

The "child" archetype represents immaturity and dependency—the overbearing need to seek comfort and security from others and the inability to think independently. Although this is how we all begin as children, adults can also manifest this archetype through overdependence on others. People with the child archetype follow the crowd and need constant external validation. As a result, they never stand out or develop their authentic selves. Overcoming the child archetype requires developing the spiritual qualities of *independence* and *self-reliance*. You must learn to think on your own and grow out of the conditioned beliefs instilled by parents, culture, religious institutions, and marketing.

The "victim" archetype represents helplessness. The victim blames someone else for their problems: it's the fault of their parents, the government, the rich, or the immigrants—the list includes anyone and everyone. The victim does not see a way out of the situation, and more importantly, *doesn't want to*. Overcoming the victim archetype requires taking responsibility for your actions and working to find solutions to problems. Taking responsibility is empowering because you can now do something about your problems. The spiritual quality to develop here is *creatorhood*—the ability to exercise your power to create the life you want.

The third archetype is "the prostitute," which represents selling oneself for material gain, power, or fame. The prostitute archetype is at play when you say yes merely to please others, and when you compromise your values or integrity for material gain. The spiritual quality to work on is *self-respect*. To overcome the prostitute archetype, you must learn to value your integrity and self-worth over security or gain. When you possess healthy self-respect, you are not for sale. You stand firm for your values, regardless of outside pressure or the need for security.

The fourth archetype is "the saboteur," where you unconsciously undermine your success and happiness due to low self-esteem. Dominated by fear, you fail to work toward your true potential and, instead, settle for what feels familiar. To overcome the saboteur archetype, you must recognize your capabilities, work to overcome inner obstacles, and build confidence. The spiritual quality to develop here is *trust in your abilities*.

The four archetypes serve as valuable reflective tools for self-awareness and inner growth. By recognizing these archetypes in yourself and overcoming them, you can reach your highest potential.

Rajas (Physical or External Power)

The quest for *external power* is what drives modern society, institutions, and most people. External power is celebrated by our economic system, which rewards monetary success. At the individual level, this search underlies the need to accumulate money, possessions, influence, and political capital. At the collective level, people pursuing power organize themselves into ideological groups or nations and compete for resources, leading to struggle, conflict, violence, and even war.

In relationships, the need to dominate and win at all costs creates never-ending power struggles that are the stuff of tabloids.

Sattva (Spiritual or Internal Power)

Sattva is the highest manifestation of power—not just raw power but true spiritual power. When you align with sattva, you live a life of joy, meaning, and synchronicity. More importantly, you think about how to bring joy to the collective through creativity and service.

An example of someone with great spiritual power is Mohandas Gandhi, whose life presented a stark contrast between internal and external power. Gandhi was a frail man who, compared to other statesmen, did not possess exemplary oratory skills. Even after he became active in political life, he held no titles and owned few material possessions. When Gandhi died, his net worth was *less than nine dollars.*

To appreciate Gandhi's spiritual power, however, we must understand the colonial conditions in which he served. Gandhi lived in a country ruled and exploited by a foreign power. People in his country were poor, uneducated, and exhausted by oppression.

How could he stand against the British Empire, the mightiest force on the planet? There were two obvious choices. The first was to do nothing and tolerate oppression—the way of the coward. The second was to meet force with force—the way of the revolutionary. But using brute force would inevitably beget more force and hostility. Gandhi's genius lay in choosing a third, more evolved way—nonviolent resistance, a path that saw oppressors not as enemies but as people driven by mistaken beliefs. Guided by this profoundly simple idea, Gandhi led three hundred and forty million people to freedom. Furthermore, his ideas became the guiding light for other leaders, such as Martin Luther King Jr.

How Levels of Consciousness Manifest in Relationships

As I noted above, your level of consciousness is foundational to your relationships. When one or both partners are at the level of tamas, the relationship will be marked by abuse, victimhood, addictions, dependency, and drama. Powerlessness makes the relationship miserable.

When both partners are at the level of rajas, the relationship will be marked by power struggles, manipulation, and aggression; it becomes a battlefield.

At the highest possible level of spiritual alignment, when both partners are at the level of sattva, the relationship will be marked by harmony, shared joy, and unconditional love. It becomes a *spiritual partnership*.

The three relationship types are compared below:

	Tamas	Rajas	Sattva
Perception of Self-Worth	*I am unworthy.*	*My worth comes from power over others.*	*I am inherently worthy, and so are others.*
The Purpose of Relationships	*Others must make me feel worthy.*	*Others must do what I wish.*	*In my relationships, we all share joy and honor each other.*
Methods of Getting What I Want	*Victimhood, Blame*	*Control, Manipulation*	*Communication, Empathy, Compassion*

How to Elevate Your Relationships to Sattva

Since relationships are informed by our level of consciousness, the daily practices of meditation, self-inquiry, and spiritual study are foundational to improving our relationships. In addition, there are three keys to elevating relationships: (1) understand and transcend conditioning, (2) learn to effectively communicate your needs, and (3) invest time in relationships. Let's look at each one in turn.

Understand and transcend conditioning.

"Love is a choice, not a feeling. Feelings come and go, and if we choose to base our most important relationships on how we feel at any particular moment, we are in for a rough and rocky journey. Love is a verb, not a noun. Love is something we do, not something that happens to us."

—Matthew Kelly

Our choices, behaviors, and expectations come from conditioned patterns. The standards we set for our children depend on those our parents set for us. In relationships, this conditioning creates a prison of *shoulds* and *musts*—notions about what makes a successful relationship, the roles of partners, and even how love needs to be expressed.

In romantic relationships, for example, the notion of the ideal partner is a common form of conditioning. It drives us to think that our partner must make us feel special and fulfill our every want: emotional, financial, spiritual, and sexual. *My partner must be attractive, intelligent, successful, loving, fit, witty, and fun.* The list goes on and on.

If you give it some thought, however, you can easily see that *no human being can fulfill all these expectations,* which are not even real needs, but conditioned wants created by the media. Trapped in these expectations, people will likely keep searching for the ideal partner—jumping from relationship to relationship instead of giving love an opportunity. A new relationship might begin with strong attraction and passion, but as it progresses, differences appear. These might be about small things, such as tidiness, or big things, such as money management, politics, and sexuality. Since conditioning sees differences as threats, it turns relationships into a struggle to change others.

To see how conditioning undermines relationships, consider tidiness. If you grew up in a household where tidiness was highly valued, you are likely to value human beings based on their level of tidiness. What happens when you begin a relationship with somebody who does not highly value tidiness? Should you tell the person they are worthless because they don't tidy up their belongings as well as you'd like? If you choose your conditioning, that's what you will do. Further, you might try to change the other person by resorting to criticism, threats, and, if all else fails, force. If the other person still does not change, you might become angry, even violent.

You can choose differently, however, by *choosing love*. If you choose love, you'll realize that your standard of tidiness is merely a preference, not a must to make the relationship work.

EXERCISE
Understand Your Conditioning

1. Make a list of qualities you think you need to have in another person to have a successful relationship with them. You can focus on family, friends, or professional relationships.

2. Examine each quality and answer the following questions:

    a. Why is this quality important? Does it originate from your authentic self or from conditioning? Qualities from the authentic self, such as compassion, are spiritual in nature. Qualities from conditioning, such as having a high income or physical attractiveness, come from family or media influences.

    b. Is this quality really needed to make your relationship work?

    c. Can you think of people who do not have this quality and yet have successful relationships? Their example can help you see that conditioning places unnecessary expectations on relationships. Your relationships can be lighter and more joyous without them.

Learn to effectively communicate your needs.

While unburdening your relationships from false expectations is crucial, that does not mean you need to endure relationships that don't meet your needs. That would be a position of powerlessness, not authentic power.

The problem, however, is that we have not been taught how to communicate in a way that our needs can be met. Without the skill of effective communication, we resort to unhelpful ways of expression, such as blame, criticism, or passive-aggressive behavior, which only lead to frustration, resentment, and relationship breakdowns over time. Remember that communicating your needs is your responsibility; people cannot read minds. How unfair to expect others to fulfill your needs if you haven't clearly communicated them!

A communication framework that can transform your relationships is Nonviolent Communication (NVC), developed by psychologist Marshall Rosenberg in the 1960s. NVC is based on the idea that people are more likely to communicate effectively and compassionately when they focus on their feelings, needs, and values, and when they use non-judgmental and empathetic language. The goal is to foster mutual understanding and empathy between people, even when they disagree or have differing perspectives. This communication approach involves four key components: observations, feelings, needs, and requests.

1. Observations

The great philosopher Krishnamurti once said that *the ability to observe without judgment is the highest form of human intelligence.* Judgment is deeply embedded in our thinking. When we judge people, we use labels to box them into stereotypes: good or bad, normal or abnormal, responsible or irresponsible, smart or ignorant, and so on. In general, when we think someone is bad, we may want to punish them because that is how we're conditioned to respond. Judgment is toxic: it dehumanizes people and sows the seeds of violence against them.

Judgment prevents people from getting their needs met, which leads to frustration and the deterioration of relationships. Let's illustrate this through an example of a couple, Jim and Martha, from Rosenberg's popular book *Nonviolent Communication: A Language of Life.*

Like all couples, Jim and Martha have basic needs they would like their relationship to fulfill. Jim, however, is conditioned to think with judgment and focuses on what's wrong with Martha, rather than how to fulfill these needs. If Martha wants more affection, Jim thinks Martha is needy and dependent; if Jim wants more affection than Martha is providing, he considers her aloof and insensitive. If Martha is more concerned about details than Jim is, Jim sees her as picky and compulsive; if Jim is more concerned about details, he sees Martha as sloppy and disorganized.

Even if Jim does not communicate these labels out loud, by judging Martha, he sees her as *a problem to be fixed*. If Jim does not change this toxic way of thinking, it will destroy their relationship. If he wants to create a heart-centered connection with Martha, the first step is to observe specific actions preventing him from meeting his needs and expressing his concerns without judgment, criticism, and blame.

2. Feelings

Feelings are what make us human. When we allow ourselves to say we are scared, relieved, or delighted, we communicate at a level that touches people's hearts. Expressing our feelings, however, is difficult for two reasons. First, conditioning discourages us. Our society values analytical, masculine qualities and suppresses the emotional, feminine ones. Expressing our feelings makes us vulnerable, which we are taught to avoid. So, we make sure not to show any emotions. This is especially true for men, who have learned that to be tough, they must be unemotional—"men don't cry."

The second reason we fail to express feelings is that we are limited by language. Even when we use the word "feel," we may not really be expressing feelings. For example, consider these statements:

"I feel like a failure." *(This is an opinion.)*

"I feel that my partner is irresponsible." *(This is an evaluation.)*

"I feel ignored." *(This is an interpretation of others' actions.)*

Expressing our feelings requires us to use words that communicate the shades of our emotions. When our needs are being met, for example, we could say that we feel *satisfied, pleased, glad, or grateful*. When they are not, we could say we feel *afraid, ashamed, sad, or furious*.

3. Needs

The third component in NVC is acknowledging the source of our feelings—our needs. Our needs include safety, autonomy, respect, connection, honesty, integrity, understanding, and being nurtured. These needs must be acknowledged before they can be fulfilled, but we often do not do this for two reasons. First, we feel guilty because we've been told that it's selfish to focus on our needs. Women, in particular, have been taught that the ideal woman sacrifices her needs to take care of others. Because of this, women often ignore their needs.

NVC teaches us that our needs are not inconveniences; *they are gifts*. Humans experience joy when they willingly fulfill other people's needs. Why not give others the gift of your needs?

Further, express your needs without blaming others or yourself.

4. Requests

The final component in NVC is to make positive and specific requests (instead of vague or negative ones). When you say to your partner, "I want you to love me," what exactly are you asking them to do? Aren't you asking them to do everything required to make you feel loved? In other words, you are asking for the impossible.

Similarly, when you say, "Don't spend so much time at work," you have communicated what you don't want, not what you do want. A positive request would be, "I would like you to spend at least one evening at home with the family every week."

The key to making requests is that they should not be communicated as demands. We often make demands when speaking to people under our authority, such as subordinates or children. A demand is a threat, which tells the other person to either comply or face punishment. When people hear a demand, they get triggered and either submit or rebel. In either case, the request is seen as coercive, and recipients respond from the instinct of self-preservation, not joy.

When people do not agree to our requests, it does not mean we should give up on our needs. Instead, we can use their responses to understand their point of view. By maintaining understanding, we can often find alternate ways to fulfill each other's needs beyond the initial request.

EXERCISE
Steps to Communicating with Empathy

- What are your top three personal or professional relationships?
- Which of your needs are not being met in each relationship?
- Write down statements that express your needs.
- Tell each person your needs in a positive way.
- Listen to the other person's needs with empathy.
- Create a plan to meet each other's needs.

Invest time in relationships.

True love reveals itself not in grand gestures but in the sacred act of giving your time—the ultimate currency of care. In the modern age, however, it has become easier to prioritize work or mindless entertainment over spending time with loved ones. This is reinforced by conditioning. Men often prioritize their careers over spending time with family (and tell themselves it is for the good of their family). Women may pour into children while their relationship with their partner withers. Technology's unending assault on human attention has further strained relationships.

Relationships aren't seasonal events—they're living ecosystems requiring daily attention. The opportunities to connect can be found in simple moments: a morning breakfast without cellphones, an intentional pause to listen after work, or time spent with family every week. Ordinary, consistent acts of presence will create tiny threads of unshakable bonds.

EXERCISE
Schedule Time for Relationships

- What are your top relationships (family, friends, colleagues, etc.)?

- Create rituals to spend time with others.

   a. Set a specific time each day for distraction-free communication with loved ones; for example, taking a walk together.

   b. For all important relationships, create weekly or monthly rituals.

Relationships: An Opportunity for Kindness

Relationships provide the opportunity to cultivate kindness. Dealing with imperfect human beings and observing these imperfections (while working on our own) is a difficult lesson, one that often takes many lifetimes to master. When we are quick to judge and criticize, the toxic energy can damage the relationship. The key is to approach imperfections with compassion rather than judgment, which creates a safe space for addressing and transforming them. Perhaps an example from my life can illustrate this point.

When Aditi and I got married, we were both poor graduate students. One of Aditi's heartfelt desires was to travel the world. Although we could afford it, we would be stretching beyond our means and using up our savings. We talked about it for a while. Ultimately, Aditi decided to sacrifice her desire and, instead, save aggressively so we could buy a house.

While the savings were going as planned, I started exploring opportunities to make more money. Unfortunately, I possessed little financial acumen and an overabundance of ambition—a combination that's lethal to financial health.

I was working with someone who seemed to have good business success, so I decided to invest our savings in a venture with him. Aditi said she did not get the right vibe from him, but I told her she didn't know what she was talking about. That was a mistake I later came to regret. (Tip for men: There is an inexplicable power known as *a woman's intuition*. Swallow your pride and don't argue with it.)

The investment soured, and we lost our money. It was heartbreaking because we had sacrificed so much to save every penny. I hung my head in shame when I brought the news to my wife. She had every right to criticize me, and I knew I deserved it. I had foolishly lost what we had saved over years—while denying ourselves the simple pleasures of life. Worse, I had done it against her expressed wishes. I was shocked when Aditi said, "It's okay, honey! Sometimes things don't work out." Not a word of criticism. What's more, she has *never* brought up the matter again in our conversations.

My wife's kindness has taught me what true love is all about; it is not an emotion bound to the physical, but the quiet strength of compassionate support stretching into the spiritual.

May you, too, give and receive the spiritual support that elevates.

CLAIRE'S JOURNEY

Some spiritual journeys, though begun with good intentions, become catastrophic if the seeker lacks adequate energetic tools. Claire shares her spiritual transformation as a cautionary tale.

The spiritual path is about learning to master consciousness and energy. Like any other endeavor, you need a competent guide and tools; without them, the journey can turn into a nightmare, as it did for me.

My path began with the abrupt and chaotic opening of my "clairs" (clairvoyance and clairaudience) by a well-meaning neighbor who, for better or worse, became my first spiritual teacher. In a matter of moments, I found myself engulfed in a realm of which I knew little, without the necessary defenses or abilities to navigate this terrifying new plane. My life before then lacked spiritual practice in any meaningful way, and my "teacher" in this moment was just beginning her own spiritual journey and was therefore ill-suited to provide me with the necessary guidance to navigate what I'd been airdropped onto. Looking back at this moment, I can't help but cringe at our naivety.

Being thrown into the proverbial deep end of clairvoyance and clairaudience—and my teacher's inability to effectively guide me—led to mental breakdowns and hospitalizations, almost resulting in my being institutionalized in a psychiatric hospital. It ultimately left me unable to function in the technological world to which I was accustomed.

The state in which I found myself after these gifts were revealed greatly juxtaposed with my affluent and privileged upbringing on America's East Coast. Aside from my sister regaling me with stories of reincarnation and my family's obligatory prayer before dinner, my upbringing was devoid of religion or spirituality. My family admonished "West Coast people" as weird and New Age. In fact, it wasn't until the year before college, while at boarding school, that I met anyone I would even consider as having a liberal or spiritual way of thinking.

Before my premature initiation into the world of spirituality, I wandered lustfully from place to place—exploring the world, attending Cornell briefly, living in Switzerland for a semester, traveling across Europe, and staying with a friend in England for a spell. I lived in Portland, Chicago, and Seattle, and skied the slopes of Colorado until earning my degree in political science. After completing graduate school, my husband and I moved to California's Napa Valley while I worked at a local winery. However, the cost of living was unsustainable, and we spent the next seven years living in Portland, Oregon, where I worked in the field of technology.

My life of curiosity settled into a routine of work and climbing the corporate ladder. I became a workaholic and had little time for such things as spirituality. I did find time to read books by Brian Weiss and considered myself open to learning more. But my focus remained decidedly on work.

During the COVID lockdowns of 2020, when I was offered a healing and opening by my neighbor, I naively jumped at the chance, utterly unprepared for the abrupt transformation that would take place.

Within a matter of moments, my entire worldview changed fundamentally. I heard voices, *too many voices*. I couldn't control it, turn it down, or turn it off. I could no longer work or even function effectively. After an extended stay in the hospital stemming from the influence of dark spirits, my husband was advised to place me in a psychiatric hospital. Luckily, he refused, and though I did see a psychotherapist who medicated me with psychotropic drugs, I also sought the aid of spiritual teachers and healers.

After finding solace in the works of Steve Noble and being taught to free myself of dark energies by Louisa Havers, I was able to return to work. But I found living a life surrounded by technology did little for my spiritual growth. What's more, my superiors, having little sympathy for what I was contending with, tasked me with the workload ordinarily required of three people, and I was soon mentally drowning in the cult of corporate. I have since left that job and have no intention of returning.

After spending thousands of dollars on genuine healers as well as connoisseurs of snake oil, I found Dr. K Narayan and Children of Infinity. I now know that this guidance could have very well saved me from losing my mind and seeing all joy drained from my life. Indeed, I was attempting to build my spiritual future on sand without so much as a hammer in my spiritual tool belt. I began to work backwards, seeking the knowledge I'd need to continue this path. Having been taken advantage of and my best-laid plans gone astray, I was distrustful of Dr. Narayan and fearful of being spiritually hurt again. Still, I plowed ahead with a deep desire to find a community of spiritual people, heal my brain, and fix the impact my chaotic opening had on my spiritual health.

I exchanged daily psychotropic medication for daily spiritual meditation. I have detoxed myself from social media and no longer spend time with powerless people. I have accepted the concept of Essentialism—meaning, to stop searching and instead focus on creating a daily pattern to support finding my soul purpose. For the first time in a very long time, I am hopeful for my spiritual future.

I hope mine is a cautionary tale that underscores the need to build a solid spiritual foundation instead of becoming enamored with psychic abilities. Many on the spiritual path get distracted with spiritual power or even harmless curiosity, which delays them on the journey and can create disasters.

I encourage those who relate to my story to begin their journey safely and in the company of those capable of guiding them. I will leave you with an African proverb I feel says it best: "If you want to go fast, go alone; if you want to go far, go together." I pray that you journey together with kindred souls.

Claire (name changed) retired from a career in technology. She is a volunteer and community facilitator for Children of Infinity.

Step 11: Pursue Joy

"Joy is the holy fire that keeps our purpose warm and our intelligence aglow."

—Helen Keller

"Joy does not simply happen to us. We have to choose joy and keep choosing it every day."

—Henri Nouwen

The words *pleasure, happiness,* and *joy* are often used interchangeably—yet each carries a distinct essence and shapes our lives differently. To live with greater depth and intention, we must understand how they differ.

Pleasure is of the body—a fleeting delight derived from fulfilling biological needs. When you eat a delicious cake, it satisfies the biological drive of hunger. A warm bath or a soothing touch all deliver instant gratification. But like a spark, pleasure burns bright and fast. Pleasure's fleeting nature doesn't mean it's bad, only that it's momentary.

Happiness is of the psyche. It's a glow that comes from progress and achievement. Getting what you want can create a state of euphoria, especially if you've overcome challenges to earn it. I still remember the first car I bought as a graduate student. I saved every month for a year to buy a twelve-year-old Toyota Corolla, and when I finally bought it, I felt like I had bought a private jet. The car wasn't just a possession; it represented something priceless: independence. No longer did I need to rely on my car-owning friends to go to HEB, the local grocery store in Austin.

The euphoria lasted only a month, however, after which I felt like just another graduate student with a car.

In psychology, this phenomenon is called *hedonic adaptation*—the initial emotional effect of a significant life event (whether positive or negative) diminishes over time, and people generally return to their previous level of happiness.

Here's the crucial realization: happiness is *socially conditioned*. Depending on where you live, owning just one car can make you happy or unhappy, not because owning a car is inherently a source of happiness, but rather because it's a reference point to compare yourself with others. If you lived in the village where I was born, where no one had a car, you'd feel ecstatic. If you lived in suburban United States, with everyone around owning multiple cars, you'd feel wanting. Notice that what brings you happiness or unhappiness has no inherent merit. It's always dependent on comparing, often unconsciously, what you have with what others have.

In contrast to pleasure and happiness, joy is of the spirit. Joy is not about acquiring or accomplishing; it's the quiet radiance of self-expression that is independent of circumstances. When you create music for the love of it, for example, you channel your authentic self. Your music may not bring you social recognition or money, but the process of creating is its own reward.

The pursuit of joy encompasses two interrelated paths, often referred to as the yin and yang in philosophical traditions. The first path, *the path of action*, or the outward path, is pursued by aligning your actions with your authentic self. The second path, *the path of being*, or the inward path, is about recognizing that joy is an inner state always available to you, independent of external circumstances.

Let's delve into these two paths, starting with the outer path of acting upon your highest excitement.

The Outer Path: Do What You Enjoy

Activities that enable us to express our true selves bring us tremendous joy. The outer path is about organizing our time and energy to pursue these activities consciously and systematically, which eventually leads to mastery.

What brings you joy is unique to you and needs to be pursued for its own sake. An activity that brings me joy, for example, is playing musical instruments. I adored music from an early age, but growing up in India, I did not have access to formal music lessons. When I turned fourteen, my father brought me a small Casio keyboard. I began teaching myself how to play popular songs by ear. The hours of playing drove my parents crazy; they eventually gave me headphones, so they didn't have to listen to my constant cacophony. The long, arduous process of learning to play songs this way took many years, but I became good at it. When I turned 22, I finally got access to a teacher and learned how to read music.

When I began creating videos for Children of Infinity, I wanted to add intro and outro music to them. I could have used stock music, but I took the opportunity to pursue my joy by learning music composition. I admit that my music is nowhere near a professional level, but creating it brings me tremendous joy.

We have been hearing the advice "follow your heart" since we were kids. Why then don't we just do what we enjoy? There are two reasons.

The first is the conditioned belief that joy is a frivolous pursuit, unsuited for adults. Growing up, we heard parents and teachers demand that we focus on studies and grades instead of play. We were taught that grown-ups are responsible people who work hard to support their families—a notion heavily propagated by the media, which depicts adults as people devoted to financial success and family responsibilities, not to carefree play. This conditioning confines our vision to the narrow, utilitarian aspect of life—money and success, instead of joy.

The second reason is that pursuing joy requires time, energy, and discipline. When we lack a strong motivation, we find it easy to sacrifice joy for passive entertainment.

But you don't need to rely on strong willpower; there is an easier way to invest in joy: develop friendships with others who are passionate about what brings you joy. There is nothing more delightful than finding others with the same passion and making joy a communal experience. It is because of a feeling of camaraderie that members of sports teams and music bands form lifelong bonds with each other.

With the internet, connecting with like-minded people has become easier than ever. Spend some time researching communities in your local area. Once you find a community you like, become an active participant and, even better, contribute time to supporting that community.

EXERCISE
Do What You Enjoy

1. What activities bring you joy?

2. Schedule time to dedicate at least 30 minutes every day to the activity that gives you the most joy.

3. Become an active participant in a community that can support your joy.

The Inner Path

A commitment to living with joy requires a fundamental shift: Joy lies within, not outside. We must become active co-creators of our experience and remove obstacles to experiencing joy within.

The inner path to joy requires changing ourselves so we can experience joy *regardless of circumstances*—without buying a fancy home, making more money, or finding a better partner. This shift can liberate us. Instead of sacrificing the present moment to get something or to be somewhere else, we can enjoy it *without needing to change it.* This includes enjoying all aspects of our life: work, relationships, and even chores.

Enjoying Work

Working constitutes the single largest expenditure of time in our lives. Given the large investment, wouldn't it make a tremendous difference if you enjoyed your work?

"That depends on what the work is," you might respond.

Aren't some kinds of work inherently more enjoyable than others? Isn't being a surgeon, whose work provides a rare combination of challenge, money, and helping others, more enjoyable than being a lowly industrial welder?

To answer the question, let's examine research by renowned psychologist Dr. Mihaly Csikszentmihalyi, who spent his life researching *peak experiences,* which are periods of such intense engagement that time seems to slow down, and your entire being becomes one with the experience. Athletes and musicians often experience this state, which is also called *being in the zone.*

Dr. Csikszentmihalyi interviewed about 200 welders in a railroad assembly plant in Chicago. The workers endured long, physically demanding hours in a grueling environment, bearing uncomfortable temperatures and incessant metal clanging. When it was time to clock out, the welders understandably sought to forget the drudgery through drinks at nearby saloons, followed by hours of television at home.

Yet, among these men, the researchers found Joe Kramer, a welder with frequent peak experiences at work. Joe had been at the plant for 30 years and had taught himself every phase of its operation. He could fix anything in the plant, from a tiny electronic monitor to a huge mechanical crane. He'd declined promotions because he felt uncomfortable being a boss, yet he was the most important person at the plant.

What is the key to enjoying work, even if it is as harrowing as industrial welding? The answer is to invest spiritual energy (or, as Dr. Csikszentmihalyi calls it, *psychic energy*) into work. By elevating work into a spiritual enterprise and imbuing it with beauty, it becomes a means of expressing ourselves. In Joe's case, he saw his work not as work but as a challenging pathway to mastery (in his case, the mastery of machinery).

Of course, honoring our work as a means of spiritual growth is an old idea. Martin Luther King Jr. aptly said:

> If it falls your lot to be a street sweeper, sweep streets like Michelangelo painted pictures, sweep streets like Beethoven composed music, sweep streets like Leontyne Price sings before the Metropolitan Opera. Sweep streets like Shakespeare wrote poetry. Sweep streets so well that all the hosts of heaven and earth will have to pause and say: "Here lived a great street sweeper who swept his job well."

Enjoying Leisure

Research reveals a counterintuitive finding that peak experiences are *more likely to occur at work than at leisure*. This is because work offers the essential components of engagement: structure, challenge, and feedback.

Leisure, on the other hand, often lacks structure and challenge. To be engaging, leisure also requires an investment of spiritual energy.

The point is this: learning to invest spiritual energy in whatever we do, whether work or leisure, is a learned habit. Once we have the habit, we stop drawing boundaries between work and leisure, and it becomes a natural way of being.

In Joe's case, he used leisure to build a rock garden at his home. The garden featured an intricate arrangement of terraces and paths among hundreds of flowers and shrubs, and a sprinkler system that created a rainbow. Since Joe could not find sprinkler heads to create the fine mist needed for the rainbow, he designed them himself and built the system in his basement. He also installed floodlights holding enough of the sun's spectrum so he could enjoy rainbows at night.

Enjoying Chores

With creativity, *even the most tedious chores can be made fun.*

Let me give you an example. My daughter Aadya is very energetic and does not enjoy sitting still. When she was younger, while eating, she would play, get up, move around, and chat incessantly with her older sister. She could easily take an hour to finish a simple meal.

The worst part was breakfast, where her long mealtime made everyone late and became a source of daily stress. We tried encouragement, reason, and eventually the carrot-and-stick approach, but nothing worked.

The breakthrough came when, one night, I read her the story of Mrs. Piggle-Wiggle, an endearing character created by Betty MacDonald in the 1950s. In the story, a girl named Mary Lou runs away from home because she cannot bear washing dishes. Mrs. Piggle-Wiggle invites her in for tea and cookies. When Mary Lou tells her she hates washing dishes, Mrs. Piggle-Wiggle engages her in a game where they must wash and clean the dishes and make the kitchen spotless because, at the strike of the clock, an evil witch will visit to ensure everything is sparkling. Mary Lou plays along and enjoys the fun with Mrs. Piggle-Wiggle. Then Mrs. Piggle-Wiggle excuses herself. As the clock strikes, a witch does appear, eager to inspect the kitchen. Mary Lou is scared at first, but then she sees that, under the costume, it is Mrs. Piggle-Wiggle! The "witch" scrutinizes the plates, gives Mary Lou a pass, and retires upstairs. The whole episode is so funny that Mary Lou is instantly cured of her disdain for washing dishes.

When Aadya sat down to eat breakfast the next day, I set a timer and told her that as soon as the timer buzzed, a witch would come by to inspect whether she had finished eating. Aadya instantly busied herself in pursuing a single goal: to make the witch happy. When the timer went off, the witch came by to inspect (it was just me with Aadya's purple witch hat on). This routine continued every day at breakfast and sometimes at dinner. Although the witch's costume and entry could be significantly better, Aadya enjoyed the routine so much that she started finishing breakfast quickly. The visits from the witch happened only occasionally after, to check activities Aadya procrastinated on.

EXERCISE
Enjoy What You Do

Write down your answers to the following questions:

1. What opportunities for mastery does your work offer? How about your industry at large?

2. What goal can you set for yourself that can be achieved using your leisure time? How can you structure your leisure time to progress consistently toward that goal?

3. What daily activities do you find most boring? How can you turn those activities into opportunities for fun?

STEFENIE'S JOURNEY

What is holding you back from accepting your gifts? Stefenie's story shows us that often the first step in spiritual transformation is allowing yourself to discover who you are and how to use the gifts already within you.

On April 23, 2018, a madman drove his van onto the sidewalks of the North York City Business Centre in Toronto, ultimately killing eleven people. Had I not listened to my intuition, I might have been among the dead.

A few minutes before the attack, I was walking to the bank, as I often did during the 24 years I had worked as a law clerk in the area. Ordinarily, I would never walk through the subway tunnel on such a beautiful spring day, but on this day, a spiritual guide I'd sensed since I was a child urged me to change my path. So, I walked through the subway tunnel instead. When I came out on the other side, I felt the shock and panic of the victims on the pavement.

Although I had avoided the tragedy, it still shook me to the core. I was living a good life with my family and enjoyed my job, yet I now realized how fragile life is and how tragic it would be to die without having lived my purpose. I knew I had to prepare myself to fulfill the purpose for which I was saved. The small, still voice within that had saved my life opened the door to my spiritual transformation.

I was born in the Jamaican countryside to a family of energy intuitives. My grandmother and mother both felt energy—and so could I. It seemed quite natural to me when I was a child, but, being brought up in the Pentecostal church by my grandmother, I had to suppress my gifts for fear of blasphemy. I learned that little Christian girls should not have the budding gifts of clairvoyance or premonition. While it was within the realm of social mores in Jamaica to encounter spirits, those in communication with those spirits were seen as demonic. Lacking any spiritual outlet outside of Christianity, I put my gifts in a drawer and forgot about them.

Following the attack, I started allowing my greater power and intuition to come to the forefront of my being. In turn, I was shown the strength of my abilities. My intuition told me that my purpose was to help others transform their consciousness.

To learn more about transformation and how I could guide others, I enrolled in a heart-centered life coaching program. The program was helpful, but before I could help others, I realized that I suffered from deep insecurity.

My spirit guides spent the next six months trying to help me stamp out my insecurities and appreciate the power of my gifts. I began to experience a marvelous play of synchronicity. As I put forth questions, I was soon given answers. Information would flow to me through books, people, or the internet. As I was shown more and more, I began to trust myself. My ability to tune into the energy of others also grew. In fact, when the COVID pandemic happened, I could energetically sense the fear that engulfed my fellow church members—something I couldn't reconcile. How can one simultaneously accept the unconditional love of God and still live in fear? I realized my Christian faith had brought me as far as it could. It was time to give myself entirely to my intuition and commit to an inner spiritual path.

I jumped heart first into my spiritual transformation. My spiritual growth accelerated in the fall of 2022. It was as if I had gone to bed one night and woken up changed. I began to receive intuitive downloads about how to navigate the human journey and help others do the same.

At that time, what I most longed for was fellowship and belonging to a community. That is when I found Children of Infinity. The platform encouraged me to embrace who I am and to accept my spiritual gifts. The lectures and courses gave me a better understanding of spirituality. I finally found the science to match my experiences.

As I listened to my intuition, I was guided to speak to specific people. I now know my abilities are not uncommon, and intuition is our birthright. Every one of us is a spiritual being with gifts waiting to be nurtured. Once we accept our divine nature, everything else begins to make sense. We see the gifts that so many of us ignore and suppress as important tools to serve and bring light to others.

Stefenie Lazarus is an Intuitive Transformation and Executive Coach who helps professionals unlock their gifts and create a purposeful, fulfilling life. Her website is www.stefenielazarus.com.

Step 12: Serve

"The best way to find yourself is to lose yourself in the service of others."

—Mahatma Gandhi

"Human progress is neither automatic nor inevitable... Every step toward the goal of justice requires sacrifice, suffering, and struggle; the tireless exertions and passionate concern of dedicated individuals."

—Martin Luther King Jr.

As we progress on the spiritual path, we eventually reach a significant marker—we transcend *egocentrism*. Within the confines of egocentrism, we can't see beyond the purview of our narrow interests, which supersede the interests of others. We may spend our entire lives gathering and protecting resources for ourselves and our families.

After evolving past egocentrism, we begin to see ourselves as part of the whole, with our well-being inextricably linked with that of others. To enhance collective well-being, reduce suffering, and bring joy to others, we willingly seek opportunities to serve. We dedicate our resources to more significant causes than our narrow self-interest. By devoting ourselves to service, our incarnation fulfills its highest purpose—to transform our collective reality into a vibrant manifestation of love.

Service: Why, What, and How

Learning *why* to serve is as important as learning *how* to serve. The spiritual foundation of my teachings is oneness—that all sentient beings are portions of Source and, thus, are our *siblings*. Whether they speak our language, see the world as we do, or even understand oneness is immaterial—they are still our siblings. Their suffering is our suffering, and their joy our joy. To contribute to the well-being and upliftment of our kin is an opportunity and honor.

What differentiates true service is that it's offered *without expecting anything in return*. Such an offering carries the vibration of unconditional love, which heals, spreads joy, and elevates. Many people, however, serve only for personal gain—either directly in the forms of money, power, and influence, or indirectly through the intangibles of prestige, publicity, and fame.

We are biologically wired to seek survival, safety, and security, but service requires evolving beyond those lower objectives into the divine territory of empathy, compassion, and unity. At higher states, we serve out of love, not for gain. An example of this is a mother's love for her baby. A mother goes through considerable inconvenience and physical discomfort to take care of her baby. Does the mother do so because she expects something from the baby? No. She cares for the baby out of love. Similarly, when we are guided by love, we unlock the ability to serve without expecting anything in return.

Giving Away Time and Money

We can begin serving by giving our time and money to worthy causes. Giving is a spiritual principle that operates at all levels in the universe: the universe has given us the gifts of life and free will. Giving has deep psychological, emotional, and spiritual benefits. Studies by psychologists show that spending money on others may bring greater happiness than spending money on yourself. When given with the right spirit, even a small amount of money (five dollars in one study) can boost your happiness.

But we don't need elaborate studies to understand how fulfilling giving is; we know it intuitively. Giving puts us in the spiritual energy of abundance, and we signal to the universe that we have progressed in our evolution and are ready to focus on the needs of others.

Why Don't We Give?

Many people don't give consistently because they see giving as *a loss* (which we are biologically wired to avoid). Of course, humans tend to cover up underlying reasons and use excuses that sound valid. The most common reasons people tell themselves to justify withholding are:

1. Lack: "I just don't have any money or time to give."

The truth is, giving away a little of our resources would hardly affect our lifestyle. Considering that we all have resources consumed by the quadrant of waste (see Step 8), why not take some of those resources and give them away?

2. Paralysis: "I believe in so many causes—I don't know which one to support."

As the saying goes, *Don't boil the ocean.* Instead, start small with one cause you can support today.

3. Lack of trust: "Most of the money nonprofits receive is wasted on paying wages."

While this might be true for some nonprofits, it's not true for most of them. Most nonprofits are driven by people dedicated to a cause. They have sacrificed a more comfortable lifestyle to work in the non-profit sector.

4. Skepticism: "It wouldn't make a real difference."

Giving even a small amount can make a huge difference in someone's life. According to Children International, a global nonprofit organization, it takes a mere $39 a month to provide children in a third-world country with life-changing interventions, such as access to medical care, education, and job training before graduation. *You can transform a life for less than the cost of a single meal at a fancy restaurant.*

Do not let excuses deprive you of the joy of giving.

The 1% Solution

The simplest way to overcome fear of loss is to take small, purposeful steps. If you lack a giving practice, begin by committing a small amount of resources, such as giving an hour each week and one percent of your income every month. The small amount will not affect your lifestyle. In addition, since charitable giving is tax-deductible, it really costs you even less than what you give.

Believe in a Cause

When we believe in a cause, giving to that cause becomes effortless. Here is how you can set up a giving practice:

1. Examine your life and consider how charity from others has made a difference in your life.

2. Find at least *one cause* you believe in wholeheartedly. Find a nonprofit that serves that cause. Don't be afraid to ask the organization how they will use your donation.

3. Find how you can donate an hour of your time every week. With easy access to virtual tools, you can contribute to organizations across the globe. Finding a local organization, however, might be better for fostering in-person connections.

4. Set up an automated program to donate one percent of your monthly income to a non-profit.

5. Review your charitable giving after a year, and when you do so, check in with yourself: *Can I give more?*

Service

In addition to donating your resources to existing organizations, you can also start your own. You will not only bring light and love to your fellow beings but also creater bigger impact by letting others be a part of your vision. Be aware, however, that creating an organization comes with challenges, the most powerful among them being the ever-present influence of ego, which seeks not to serve but to gain.

The Path of Service: A Story

Let me illustrate how the journey of service might unfold through the story of Jim, a fictitious hero. This story incorporates lessons I've learned through my own experience, while also observing others on the path of service.

Jim grew up in an abusive household and had trouble with school and relationships. Fortunately, he came across a meditation teacher in his late twenties and experienced a profound inner transformation due to the shift in his awareness. He then saw that his calling is to share the gift of transformation with others.

THE PHASE OF STRUGGLE

Jim decides to embark on the path by teaching meditation to people in his community. When he begins this noble cause, he is unaware that he starts the journey burdened with *the weight of expectations.*

One of Jim's friends offers him a space to host a small gathering. Jim advertises the event on social media and Meetup, where many people express interest and promise to attend.

The day of Jim's first meditation class arrives. He and his friend wait to greet newcomers. The event is supposed to start at 7 p.m., but nobody is there yet. Finally, at 7:15, Jim realizes that no one will show up. His heart sinks.

But Jim is unwilling to give up. He puts much more effort into promoting his event, and some people show up the next week. They thank Jim for his insights and generosity. Among them is Bradley, who is so excited that he promises to bring two of his friends next time. He also offers to help with anything Jim needs.

This progress excites Jim. He can envision a heart-centered community of dozens of people. He can barely wait to see what happens next week.

When the next week comes, however, Bradley is nowhere to be found, and neither is anyone who attended his meditation the previous week.

Jim now begins to doubt himself, his work, and those he's trying to serve. Why, he asks himself, is he pouring his heart into trying to help people who can't even keep simple promises? Maybe this is a foolish quest, after all. Or maybe he just doesn't have the charisma to hold people together. Is the effort worth it?

Jim has encountered discouragement, which is the first obstacle on the path of service. Unbeknownst to him, the burden of expectations is wearing him down. He is trying to measure his service through external results, such as the number of people eager to receive his gift. If Jim wants to continue this journey, he needs to abandon expectations and stop counting and measuring. He must realize that the value of his work can't be measured by how many people show up, but only by the purity of intent with which he serves.

THE PHASE OF GROWTH

Jim decides that serving even a few people is worth making the effort. Thus, he overcomes discouragement and moves forward.

A few months pass, and a community starts growing around him. People can feel that he serves from his heart, and they are attracted to the light he carries. Jim now faces the next phase of problems—ones that require him to grow.

Mary, a meditation group member, asks Jim if he has a nonprofit so she can write off a donation. The problem is that Jim doesn't know how to set one up.

To support members, Jim needs a bigger space, but he doesn't know whom to ask for donations, or how.

A veteran member complains to Jim that a newcomer is soliciting others for his private healing practice, but Jim hasn't set up a code of conduct for members. Furthermore, being a low-key guy, Jim doesn't like confrontation. He needs to set clear expectations for how members should interact with each other and call out behavior that violates guidelines.

Sue, a member of Jim's community, invites him to share about his work on her podcast. It turns out that Jim does not have good speaking skills—he mumbles, and his voice lacks confidence.

Jim wonders how he can ever accomplish what he needs to put the nonprofit on sound footing, much of which feels like bureaucracy. He doesn't remember signing up for this. He sometimes wonders if he should close the shop and focus on his own enlightenment instead.

Jim is running into the second obstacle on the path of service—the inability to grow out of his comfort zone. To continue his mission, he will have to master what feels unfamiliar today—leadership, resource management, communication skills—and set a larger vision for his community. Though these are opportunities for him to grow, they also make him uncomfortable.

What's more, pushing through one's comfort zone is not a one-time event but a lifelong commitment. At every stage of service, there are opportunities to progress from *what is* to *what can be*, and each requires stretching oneself in unfamiliar and uncomfortable ways.

THE PHASE OF SUCCESS

Jim accepts the challenges of growth and works to improve his leadership and communication skills. As a result, his community flourishes. In fact, as the need for his guidance grows, he opens many centers around the nation. He now runs into the third phase of challenges: those that come with success.

Scott, a smooth-talking local politician, tells Jim that he wants to donate money to Jim's nonprofit, and he hints that he expects Jim to tell his community to vote for him.

A local news channel wants to interview Jim. The news channel is known to promote divisive political agendas. If Jim agrees to be interviewed, he is likely to be asked to express his political views, which risks creating a rift in his organization.

Through a network of spiritual teachers, Jim meets Charlie, a charismatic communicator who has created a large following of influential and high-paying students. Charlie lives a lavish and charmed life as a celebrity. Jim wonders if it's time to cash in on his community; after all, he has served selflessly for many years—doesn't he deserve some recognition and a better lifestyle?

In this third phase of service, Jim faces the biggest obstacle he has encountered so far: distractions. These distractions can cause him to abandon the path of selfless service for the path of ego. He has to guard against "shiny objects" such as personal gain, influence, and power. If Jim has the internal strength to stay true to his higher purpose, he will become an embodiment of true service, a rare gift to humanity. Though Jim may not become widely known, he will have a lasting influence on the lives he touches. Furthermore, his guiding light will inspire the next generation of leaders to continue the work he has begun.

Lessons from Jim's Story

In Jim's story, the journey of service has three phases: struggle, growth, and success. Although Jim faces different challenges in each phase, there's just one essential quality that helps him to overcome them: an unwavering commitment to the mission. By staying committed, Jim acquires skills, avoids distractions, and develops the leadership abilities needed to accomplish his mission.

Let's do an exercise to help you on your own journey of service:

1. **Phase I: Struggle**

    a. Get a new journal and make it your *Mission Journal*. Do all your mission-related thinking and planning in this journal.

    b. Translate your intention to serve into a *mission statement* that will guide you. (For example, my mission is to raise planetary consciousness.) Keep the statement to one sentence and write it down in your *Mission Journal*.

    c. If you have not already started your journey of service, think of *one* way you can serve. Resist the temptation to think of too many ways you may offer service—just focus on one for now.

    d. What commitments would you need to serve without expecting anything in return?

    e. Stay committed to your mission despite challenges, temptations, and the complexity of dealing with human beings. Enlist peers and mentors to act as your accountability partners. Meet with them regularly to discuss your mission and your progress. Sincerely seek feedback and implement it.

2. **Phase II: Growth**

   f. What growth must you undergo to serve and fulfill the mission?

   g. What discomforts prevent you from growing? Are you willing to step out of your comfort zone?

   h. What qualities and skills must you develop to serve at your highest potential?

3. **Phase III: Success**

   i. What distractions do you face on your journey of service?

   j. Create a daily ritual to focus on your mission instead of the myriad traps of ego that success can conjure. You can do this by spending 15 to 30 minutes per day reflecting on whether you are still aligned with your mission. Review your mission before you make any important decisions. Will the decision help you serve the mission, or will it distract you?

Conclusion: Become an Instrument of Light

The yearning for transformation is so deeply ingrained in the human spirit that it has informed a universal template for storytelling. Called the "Hero's Journey," the template was popularized by Joseph Campbell in his book *The Hero with a Thousand Faces* (1949).

My favorite telling of the hero's journey is *The Matrix*, a 1999 science fiction film. The film tells the story of Neo, a computer hacker who suspects that something is fundamentally wrong with his reality but doesn't exactly know what that is.

What distinguishes *The Matrix* from other excellent science-fiction classics is its exploration of spiritual themes, such as freedom, beliefs, and human potential. Let me highlight two defining moments from the movie that are relevant to our quest for spiritual transformation.

The first moment occurs when Neo confronts the choice between the comfort of the familiar and the uncertainty of the unknown. This decision is symbolized by the scene in which Morpheus, Neo's mentor, offers him the choice between the blue pill and the red pill. By choosing the red pill, Neo embraces self-discovery and truth over security.

Upon taking the red pill, Neo awakens to a stark and unsettling reality: a world ruled by machines where humans are powerless. In this new existence, every interaction with the machine-controlled reality carries the peril of encountering *agents*—relentless, superhuman programs designed to enforce the system's control. Neo learns that agents are forces to be evaded at all costs: everyone who has ever faced them has perished.

As Neo evolves, however, he reaches a turning point when he chooses the unthinkable—to stand and fight an agent rather than flee. The moment is marked by the iconic words from Morpheus: "He is beginning to believe."

These two moments symbolize Neo's monumental growth from a novice to a master. At their core, those moments underscore the fundamental choice that you and I face as humans—the choice between security and growth. In every rendering of the hero's journey, the hero chooses growth. As modern heroes on the quest to realize our revolutionary potential, we must do the same.

Along the journey to your transformation, you will face your own agents: limiting beliefs, disempowering habits, resistance, inertia, and the biologically informed preference for comfort over meaning. Early on in the journey, these foes seem insurmountable, but when you finally face them, you will find—just as Neo did—that these foes are but illusions.

Each of us is a unique strand of Source Energy, carrying within us light that can transform not only our individual lives but the entire world. The first step to cultivating the light within is consistent spiritual practice. These practices—meditation, self-inquiry, and spiritual study—widen the channel so as to let more light through, leading to enhanced awareness and empowered living.

As our awareness grows, we begin to hear the call of our higher purpose—our dharma. Aligning with our dharma enables us to transcend our limited human capability and gain a powerful ally on the journey: the universe. This partnership accelerates the process of cultivating our unique gifts, enabling us to express ourselves fully and to experience joy.

As more light emanates from our being, we uncover opportunities to share it through service. True service, which is an outpouring of unconditional love, heals and blesses everyone it touches. Through service, we fulfill our highest calling, which is to elevate the consciousness of those around us.

I wish you the very best on your spiritual journey. May you become a beacon of light and transform our planet.

—Dr. K Narayan

Appendix: The Lightworker's Journey

The lightworker's journey has four stages. The goals and challenges for each stage are outlined below.

Beginner: A beginner lacks consistent spiritual practice. This is common when one starts the journey. However, one can stay a beginner even after decades on the spiritual path if one becomes stuck in the learning loop and fails to cultivate practices. Here are the *three major challenges* you face as a beginner lightworker:

1. **Avoiding information addiction.** There is just too much information out there, and ninety-nine percent of it is junk. Your task is to differentiate signal from noise and quickly get the knowledge that can change your life.

2. **Developing a practice routine.** One thing that keeps beginners stuck is the learning loop—a variation of information addiction. I was a victim of the learning loop for years. I would read a book, and then, instead of applying what I had learned, I would read another book, and then another. I did that because consuming information is much easier than

doing the actual work. It took me years to realize that what changes our lives is not knowledge, but practice. Cultivating spiritual practice requires trying different things, finding what works for you, and establishing habits. That's not as easy as reading a book, but you must do the work to create a strong foundation.

3. **Staying Motivated.** Inner work is difficult, and initially, progress is slow. Your task is to continue your practice, even when you don't see results. It's like going to the gym. In the initial days, all you experience is soreness. You have to persist through the discomfort before you see results. In this phase, having a supportive community makes a world of difference.

Practitioner: At this stage, your goal is to *heal yourself.* Healing is not merely about removing pathology but about achieving wholeness, a state where your authentic spiritual power begins to manifest. Here are the three challenges you face as an intermediate lightworker:

1. **Finding Transformative Technology.** True healing is an energetic (rather than an intellectual) process. To heal all aspects of your being, you need a powerful yet simple technology that works for you.

2. **Healing Limiting Beliefs.** Your limiting beliefs prevent you from becoming whole. These might be beliefs about self-worth, abundance, or your potential. You need a safe space to uncover those beliefs so you can heal them.

3. **Specific guidance.** Depending on your blocks to healing, you need specific guidance from a teacher or healing community. You will need to find the guidance that works for you.

Beacon: At this stage, your goal is to *develop and share your unique gifts*. Here are the three challenges you face as an intermediate lightworker:

1. **Connecting with your Higher Self rather than your ego.** The word *ego* stands for the false self, which is created from conditioning. It's all the false beliefs and the voice in your head. If you want to do the work of light, you need to connect with your Higher Self, which is the nonphysical aspect of your being. Your Higher Self is the inner wisdom that guides you on the human journey.

2. **Focusing on your core gift, rather than spreading yourself thin across many talents.** As wonderful as they are, spiritual possibilities can sometimes become overwhelming. Instead of being carried away, focus on your core gift and become outstanding at using it. Remember, depth matters more than breadth.

3. **Consciously pursuing the specifics of mastery, instead of attempting general improvement.** Fulfilling your purpose requires choosing specific skills and spending a deliberate effort mastering them. For example, as a spiritual teacher, I work on developing specific skills: designing courses, creating content, and delivering content. Similarly, you will have to master specific skills to fulfill your purpose.

Lighthouse: At the advanced stage of the journey, you begin to transform people's lives through tools such as books, courses, workshops, and mentorship. It is time to share your light on a massive scale. Here are the *three biggest challenges* for advanced lightworkers:

1. **Expanding your vision.** The vision that got you here won't take you higher. To make your highest contribution and play a bigger game, you must first expand your vision.

2. **Mastering leadership.** To make your highest contribution, you must stop being a lone warrior and begin duplicating yourself through leadership. You need to get others to be a part of your vision and empower them to become effective leaders, thus creating a self-sustaining force for change.

3. **Surrounding yourself with people who stretch you.** As an advanced lightworker, it's easy to surround yourself with people who admire you, but to grow, you need people who challenge you. Being part of a community of advanced lightworkers can be the biggest resource you need at this stage.

To get the tools to empower yourself on the lightworker's path, visit www.childrenofinfinity.org.

References

Introduction

Maslow, A. H. 1943. "A Theory of Human Motivation." *Psychological Review* 50 (4): 370–396.

Yogananda, Paramahansa. [1946] 1998. *Autobiography of a Yogi*. 13th ed. Self-Realization Fellowship.

Step 1

DeWitt, Richard. 2018. *Worldviews: An Introduction to the History and Philosophy of Science*. 3rd ed. Wiley-Blackwell.

Dillbeck, M. C., G. Landrith III, and D. W. Orme-Johnson. 1981. "The Transcendental Meditation program and crime rate change in a sample of forty-eight cities." *Journal of Criminal Justice* 4: 25–45.

Dillbeck, M. C. and K. L. Cavanaugh. 2016. "Societal Violence and Collective Consciousness: Reduction of U.S. Homicide and Urban Violent Crime Rates." *SAGE Open* 6 (2). https://doi.org/10.1177/2158244016637891.

Goswami, Amit. 1995. *The Self-Aware Universe: How Consciousness Creates the Material World*. Tarcher.

Hawkins, David R. 2012. *Power vs. Force: The Hidden Determinants of Human Behavior*. Hay House, Inc.

Hume, Robert E. 1921. "Chandogya Upanishad 6.1 - 6.16." In *The Thirteen Principal Upanishads*, 240-241. Oxford University Press. https://archive.org/details/thirteenprincipa028442mbp.

Ian Stevenson's important research publications on reincarnation include: *Twenty*

Cases Suggestive of Reincarnation (University of Virginia Press, 1966); *Cases of the Reincarnation Type, Vols. I-IV* (University of Virginia Press, 1975–1983); *Where Reincarnation and Biology Intersect* (Praeger Publishers, 1997); and *European Cases of the Reincarnation Type* (McFarland & Company, 2003).

The Law of One. "*The Law of One* Session 1." January 15, 1981. https://www.lawofone.info/s/1#7.

McTaggart, Lynne. 2008. *The Field: The Quest for the Secret Force of the Universe.* Harper Perennial.

Tucker, Jim B. 2005. *Life Before Life: A Scientific Investigation of Children's Memories of Previous Lives.* St. Martin's Press.

Yogananda, Paramahansa. [1946] 1998. *Autobiography of a Yogi.* 13th ed. Self-Realization Fellowship.

Step 2

Applied kinesiology is an empirical method to evaluate structural, chemical, and mental aspects of health using muscle testing. You can watch Dr. Hawkins's muscle testing demo in this video: "Dr. David Hawkins: Witness the Sacredness of all Existence." *YouTube.* https://youtu.be/rwIvyaQuvfE.

Hawkins, David R. 2012. Power vs. Force: *The Hidden Determinants of Human Behavior.* Hay House, Inc.

Law of One material is available on the L&L Research website: https://www.llresearch.org/.

Pirsig, Robert. 2008. *Zen and the Art of Motorcycle Maintenance: An Inquiry into Values.* Mariner Books Classics.

Step 3

The Children of Infinity book list is available at https://childrenofinfinity.org/recommendations/.

Christakis, Nicholas A. and James H. Fowler. 2007. "The Spread of Obesity in a Large Social Network over 32 Years." *New England Journal of Medicine* 357: 370-379.

Harari, Yuval Noah. 2014. Sapiens: *A Brief History of Humankind*. Signal Books.

McKibben, Bill. 2006. *The Age of Missing Information*. Random House.

Wu, Tim. 2017. *The Attention Merchants*. Atlantic Books.

Step 4

Newton, Michael. 2009. *Memories of the Afterlife: Life Between Lives Stories of Personal Transformation*. Llewellyn Publications.

Schwartz, Robert. 2012. *Your Soul's Gift: The Healing Power of the Life You Planned Before You Were Born*. Whispering Winds Press.

Weiss, Brian. 2001. *Messages from the Masters: Tapping into the Power of Love*. Warner Books.

Step 5

Gladwell, Malcolm. 2008. *Outliers: The Story of Success*. Little, Brown and Company.

Goyal, Singh, et al. 2014. "Meditation Programs for Psychological Stress and Well-being." *JAMA Internal Medicine*. 174 (3): 357-368.

Hölzel, Britta K, Ulrich Ott, Tim Gard, Hannes Hempel, Martin Weygandt, Katrin Morgen and Dieter Vaitl, 2008. "Investigation of mindfulness meditation practitioners with voxel-based morphometry." *Social Cognitive and Affective Neuroscience* 3: 55–61.

Narayan, K. 2025. *Heal, Transform, Ascend: Breakthrough Energy Healing from Divine Mother.* Children of Infinity.

Step 6

MacLeod, Ainslie. 2019. *The Old Soul's Guidebook: Who You Are, Why You're Here, and How to Navigate Life on Earth.* Soul World Press.

Myss, Caroline. 2003. *Sacred Contracts: Awakening Your Divine Potential.* Harmony Books.

Myss, Caroline. 2013. *Archetypes: A Beginner's Guide to Your Inner-net.* Hay House, Inc.

Step 7

Dweck, Carol S. 2007. *Mindset: The New Psychology of Success.* Ballantine Books.

Maxwell, John C. 2002. *Your Road Map for Success: You Can Get There from Here.* HarperCollins Leadership.

National Archives, Founders Online. 1743. "Poor Richard, 1743." https://founders.archives.gov/documents/Franklin/01-02-02-0089.

Step 8

Covey, Stephen R. 1989. *The 7 Habits of Highly Effective People.* Simon & Schuster.

Galloway, Stephen and Ashley Cullins. 2017. "Johnny Depp: A Star in Crisis and the Insane Story of His 'Missing' Millions." *The Hollywood Reporter,* May 10, 2017.

https://www.hollywoodreporter.com/movies/movie-features/johnny-depp-a-star-crisis-insane-story-his-missing-millions-1001513/.

Kahneman, Daniel and Angus Deaton. 2010. "High income improves evaluation of life but not emotional well-being." *PNAS* 107 (38):16489-16493. https://www.pnas.org/doi/10.1073/pnas.1011492107.

Newport, Cal. 2016. *Deep Work: Rules for Focused Success in a Distracted World.* Grand Central Publishing.

Step 9

Campbell, T. Colin and Thomas M. Campbell II. 2005. *The China Study: The Most Comprehensive Study of Nutrition Ever Conducted and the Startling Implications for Diet, Weight Loss, and Long-Term Health.* BenBella Books.

Campbell, T. Colin and Howard Jacobson. 2014. *Whole: Rethinking the Science of Nutrition.* BenBella Books.

Earth Save. "Food Choices and the Planet." n.d. https://www.earthsave.org/environment.htm.

Accessed July 22, 2025.

Ellison, Deborah L and Heather R Moran. 2021. "Vitamin D: Vitamin or Hormone?" *Nursing Clinics of North America* 56 (1):47-57. https://pubmed.ncbi.nlm.nih.gov/33549285/.

The International Agency for Research on Cancer. October 26, 2015. "IARC Monographs evaluate consumption of red meat and processed meat."

https://www.iarc.who.int/wp-content/uploads/2018/07/pr240_E.pdf

Lockley, Steven W., George C. Brainard, and Charles A. Czeisler. 2003. "High Sensitivity of the Human Circadian Melatonin Rhythm to Resetting by Short Wavelength Light," *The Journal of Clinical Endocrinology & Metabolism* 88 (9): 4502–4505.

https://academic.oup.com/jcem/article/88/9/4502/2845835

Parker-Pope, Tara and Anahad O'Connor. "Scientist Who Discredited Meat Guidelines Didn't Report Past Food Industry Ties." *The New York Times,* October 4, 2019.

https://www.nytimes.com/2019/10/04/well/eat/scientist-who-discredited-meat-guidelines-didnt-report-past-food-industry-ties.html.

Plant Based Nation. November 15, 2019. "The Comparative Anatomy of Eating." https://drmiltonmillsplantbasednation.com/the-comparative-anatomy-of-eating/.

Ratey, John J. 2008. *Spark: The Revolutionary New Science of Exercise and the Brain.* Little, Brown Spark.

Reiley, Laura. "Research group that discounted risks of red meat has ties to program partly backed by beef industry." *The Washington Post,* October 23, 2019.

https://www.washingtonpost.com/business/2019/10/14/research-group-that-discounted-risks-red-meat-has-ties-program-partly-backed-by-beef-industry/.

Step 10

Fischer, Louis. 1950. *The Life of Mahatma Gandhi.* Harper & Brothers.

Lake, Gina. 2014. *Choosing Love: Moving from Ego to Essence in Relationships.* CreateSpace.

Rosenberg, Marshall B. 2003. *Nonviolent Communication: A Language of Life.* Puddledancer Press.

Step 11

Csikszentmihalyi, Mihaly. 2008. *Flow: The Psychology of Optimal Experience.* Harper Perennial.

Frederick, S., and Loewenstein, G. (1999). "Hedonic adaptation." In *Well-being: The Foundations of Hedonic Psychology,* edited by D. Kahneman, E. Diener and N. Schwarz, 302–329. Russell Sage Foundation.

MacDonald, Betty. 1987. *Mrs. Piggle-Wiggle.* Scholastic.

SingjuPost. "Dr. MLK's 'Street Sweeper' Speech at Philadelphia School October 26, 1967." Posted January 25, 2019. YouTube. 07:30 – 08:08. https://www.youtube.com/watch?v=202nbcLwxsg.

Step 12

Dunn, Elizabeth W, Lara B Aknin, and Michael I Norton. 2008. "Spending money on others promotes happiness." *Science* 319 (5870):1687-1688. https://pubmed.ncbi.nlm.nih.gov/18356530/.

About Children of Infinity

Children of Infinity is a *transformational space* for lightworkers. The community offers guidance, tools, and fellowship to help lightworkers cultivate their gifts and reach their highest potential. To learn more about Children of Infinity and see upcoming courses and events, visit https://childrenofinfinity.org/.

About Dr. K Narayan

Dr. K Narayan has a Ph.D. in Quantum Physics and has been on the spiritual path since 1996. Through advanced energetic practices, he became a channel for Divine Mother, the source of the Divine Feminine. With assistance from Divine Mother, he creates energetic tools for spiritual transformation. He is the founder of Children of Infinity, a non-profit community dedicated to empowering lightworkers.

www.ingramcontent.com/pod-product-compliance
Lightning Source LLC
Chambersburg PA
CBHW022027050526
44107CB00096B/60